# Life Without The Shadow

Graphics and cover design by: Marianne Lindgren

Cover photos: Pixabay

Printing: IngramSpark

ISBN 978-91-519-9558-8

# Life Without the Shadow

Ralph K. Jenkins

# TABLE OF CONTENTS

# Chapter 1

## Waking Up

I would like you to imagine for a moment that you are lying on your bed and you are slowly waking up after a deep, deep, sleep. This is the first time you are waking up after being away for many years. You are contemplating what your body feels like, you are transfixed. You begin to feel a slight pressure across your legs, torso and chest; it's as if something is lying there. You have not yet opened your eyes because you are unable to. You sense the atmosphere of the space you are in and connect more deeply to the light that is passing through your eyelids. For a moment or two, you are focused on feeling your whole body and realise that you are breathing. In your mind, two questions appear that dominate your thoughts: Where am I? Who am I? A moment later I become you and you have become me.

A light, warm breeze caresses my brow and face. I feel a strong energy near me, a presence, maybe two. Light continues to pass through my eyelids and increases in strength, which helps awaken my senses. I now feel the wares of physical life as the life-force of blood runs through my veins, but I am not attached to it. In a profound way I experience how the heartbeat and the breath are connected through the electrical impulse that helps push the blood through my veins. For a moment I feel the weight of the physical body, which is restricting any movement I try to make. I try to clear my head from speculating and focus instead upon the forefinger of my right hand. I make an effort to move it. I feel my fingertip moving very slightly and then it drops. Once again, I try to move my forefinger but the effort is too great, the physical will is not there. One of my original questions came back to my mind: Where am I?

A deep calm voice sounded clearly in the chambers of my mind: *"You are resting in a heavenly place. Try to relax more deeply. Use your spiritual will to create more space in your mind, by letting go of any thoughts that appear, and breathe more deeply into your body."*

I understood that this was not my own inner thoughts. Was this telepathy? I began to follow the natural rhythm of my breath, which greatly increased my body sensations. My eyelids however remained firmly closed, but in my mind's eye,[1] I could clearly see that there was a light, a form of light, a light being that stood to my right, and another to my left. I felt warmth and peace emanating from their light pink auras. I intuitively knew that there was a strong connection between me and the two light-beings. I sent a telepathic thought out to both the beings: "Where am I?"

*"You are about to return to a Divine world in the 107th Galaxy of the third Universe."* This, telepathically from the light being on my right. There was a moment of silence. *"On an intergalactic level it is known as Earth."*

"Why? Where have I been and for how long?"

---

1  This is the spiritual third eye that holds the vibration of clairvoyance.

*"You have been in a deep intergalactic sleep, equivalent to twenty-three physical years."*

"Am I that much older now?"

*"Do not worry, you have not aged physically because there is no timeline where you have been; a vibration above the physical reality of time itself. What you have been experiencing has taken you much deeper into preparation of what is to come. Your soul has recorded everything, which will become clearer to you as you continue to follow your earth walk."* This from the other light being standing on my left.

A pressure, a force, began to build-up in my third eye. I focused and breathed through this chakra and in a matter of moments a bright light appeared and expanded; my clairvoyant vision became stronger and clearer. Now I could focus simultaneously on both light beings that were present. The one to my left flexed his wings, and I realised that he was an angel, possibly an Ark Angel. They were so majestic; illuminated, clear and sharp in their presence. Yes! The thought came running into my mind.

*"You are right, we are Ark Angels"*, responded the angel to my right.

"Why are you here with me?"

*"We and others have been watching over you for many of your lifetimes. We have come to observe your spiritual progress on this physical earth plane. You are a soul from another constellation in another Universe who has decided to continue your reincarnation on earth."*

The angel to my left responded: "*We know everything there is to know about you because nothing is hidden in accordance with Universal law.*"

I felt naked, but clean, no shadows. I understood that my Clairaudient faculty was now stronger, no problem in hearing spirit, and now I also had full clairvoyance, clear vision of spirit. These thoughts and feelings empowered me. More light came flooding into my psyche, I felt uplifted. I asked the angels: "I need some help to understand. Why I have been asleep or away in another dimension for so long?"

"*Your idea of sleep is different from ours. We never actually sleep because we do not directly have a dense physical body and a logical brain that requires rest. These are the attributes of the physical world, as you have been and still are currently experiencing. The life force that flows through us is not directly linked to the physical light that helps hold the physical body together. We are in harmony with universal consciousness and are guided by a higher vibration of light. We are the life force; we have no need of rest.*"

Wow! I wanted to know more. "Ok, then tell me, why am I in this current position, and who am I?"

"*Let's take the first question.*" This from the angel to my right.

I interrupted before they could continue. "What do I call you? Angels? You *are* angels aren't you? I mean I remember being told by many that there were beings called angels, but it never really registered, until now that is. Angels have names don't they?"

*"Yes we are angels, but not from the earth's constellation or its universe. We are from the constellation of your birthplace known as Rhjas that is in the 113,000 Galaxy of the seventh universe. I am known as Herali, to your right, the male aspect of you. And I am Relu the angel on your left, your feminine side."*

"Good, now we know each other by name", replied Herali.

"Now back to the question of why I am in this current position." I sensed Relu move a bit as even more light filled our space.

Relu answered: *"The time you have been away – 23 years - has not been noticed by your family or friends. To them it's as if you have overslept. This is because you have experienced a quantum time shift whilst journeying in your sleep state. You have had many lifetimes on earth, lived chiefly through logical perception, with a large amount of emotional stimulation and some ego, not too extreme, but none the less, ego based."*

I wanted to get up and challenge them, but I could not move an inch from where I lay. "Why can't I move?"

*"You have not yet re-entered your physical body and fully woken up"*, replied Herali.

"Is this a dream, a vision, or what?"

*"You are at this moment still receiving counselling from higher beings, such as us. You have proven by your intensions, thoughts, feelings, and love for all things that you are ready to follow a deeper path of*

*service. In this lifetime you have already taken some important initiations that have demonstrated to us that you are in harmony with universal consciousness and the laws. Now is the moment for us to unite our forces with you and to blend as one for the coming steps of your spiritual growth.*

*There is much that will change within you as you discover and experience how universal laws are the alchemy of earth's creation, the matrix. But first you can, if you wish, reflect on some of those experiences that have helped to raise your vibrations into this your next consciousness shift from the third dimension, into the fourth and eventually the fifth. These are natural steps that all souls eventually take when their emotions and ego have been, to a greater degree, transformed. Now the opportunity has come for you to initiate, which is why we are here to assist you in the positive progression of your Kundalini rising."[2]*

There was stillness and Relu continued: *"This is a natural happening that you can embrace from your heart. We are here to be of assistance and will not impose anything upon you without your full approval. You have the freedom to decide what path you wish to follow. If you say no to us, we will simply step back and continue to observe and assist you in your progress, but only when requested by your higher self. Just as we have been doing for millennia without interfering with the choices[3] you have already*

---

2  Kundalini is a natural process of energy transformation of light; some refer to it as a fire, which passes through the chakras to burn away lower forms of consciousness held within them. This helps raise their vibration towards enlightenment.

3  Choice is a logical concept of choosing between one thing and another, black or white. The act of choice creates separation. When a decision is made a third element is added, you decide for the greater good.

*made. Now it is different because you directly decided and asked for deeper knowledge, wisdom, and guidance, to live a life free from fear; to be egoless, to transform the remaining shadows, such as doubt, that cloud your way. Therefore, at this moment, you feel so clean and uplifted. You are now holding a far greater light force than you have ever done before. As your consciousness expands your entire chakra system is gradually being transformed through the Kundalini rising."*

My consciousness became blank like a blackboard waiting to be written on. Then a stream of pictures and images flew past my mind's eye; flashes of light and colour appeared and disappeared. I wanted it to stop, but I felt powerless to stop the images that continued to pass through my psychic peripheral and the deeper images that I seemed to be flying through.

*"These are the images of every thought and experiences you have had in this lifetime. You can look into the light that now appears and ask to be taken back to a moment that touched you're heart deeply."*

In that moment Herali's telepathic communication stopped, then everything else stopped too. No pictures, no images, no sound, nothing coming in. Then a small light appeared, just like the light that appeared in the middle of the black and white TV in 1960's when my dad switched it on or off. The year 1959 appeared, I was six years old. As clear as anything I could see that I was standing in the middle of a farmyard with a long milk parlour in front of me, and to my left a smaller one. To my right stood some store sheds and the dairy. These created the distinct U shape of the farmyard. I turned and looked towards the entrance of the farmyard. A small heard of cows, some twenty-one or more, were entering the yard; it was evening milking time. It was midsummer and I picked up on the cows' scent. The sounds they made was like music to me. Some of the cows rushed towards the water tank that stood in front of the main milking parlour. They were extremely thirsty due to the hot weather we were having that summer.

I got closer to the cows and watched them drink. Bulges of water ran along their windpipes like small balloons as they greedily swallowed. I was wearing wellington boots or farm boots to some, shorts and an old blue checked shirt with short sleeves. Above the bellowing of the cows, that echoed from wall to wall, I heard a clear clanging of metal that came from the dairy. I could just see the top of Iwan's head, my friend, the farmer's son. I had been helping out with the milking for just over a year now and I knew every cow by name, as well as their personality traits. I could see Robert, the farmer, waving his stick to move the few remaining cows forward into the farmyard.

The cows seemed to be very big to my little eyes, but the Hereford bull that Robert had bought a week ago, was the dominating force in the herd. I was wary of the bull that Robert had appropriately named Star because he had a white star like mark on his forehead. Unlike the cows his movements were less predictable. Robert, Iwan and I ushered the remaining cows into their allotted stalls, which was easy because each cow knew where to go. This was joy for me, to be amongst nature; somehow, I understood the plant and animal world because they talked to my heart. The dogs, chickens, ducks, sheep, and cows were my friends; companions as well as teachers. I understood that nature and its animals clearly demonstrated how life and death are but mirrors. They reminded me of something deep within, how to love unconditionally.

Relu's thoughts registered with mine again. *"We can see and understand that those moments of your life were important and helped carry you forward to explore some of the other qualities you have. If you wish you can go back into another experience that can indicate where you were in your life on a physical and spiritual level. Try to see it as a yard stick, a measurement of your natural progression of spiritual laws in Earth life."*

It was still impossible for me to move any part of my body. It was as if I were glued to the bed. I cleared my memory screen, and once more entered the void. I was now propelled to a time when I was a young man. I was eighteen years old. I had hair that touched my shoulders, to the style of the 1970's. I was wearing checked bell-bottom trousers with black, platform shoes and a green shirt that had elongated collars. I was neither a rock nor a mod. I was me. Lost. I knew I was looking for my identity, to be someone, and my Ego wanted more of it, but more of what?

Some six months prior I had passed my driving test, which was chiefly due to my brother's excellent methods of teaching me by putting me in the most difficult places to manoeuvre. Now I wanted a car, something to impress my mates with, as well as "pulling a bird or two". You know, just like my brother did with his latest girlfriend, and what I had seen on television. After all, my ego wanted to impress but I had little money, so I decided to do some extra work as a labourer on a building site to earn some money.

My brother had bought a customised Ford Anglia car which had a highly modified 1600cc engine, wide wheels, and metallic paint – purple and yellow with bucket seats and a leather racing steering wheel. Most Sunday afternoons the boys would meet at the town square to show off their highly polished possessions. My brother was one, usually accompanied by his girl-friend, and a few others with customised cars. I was captivated by a car that Marco, who was a mechanic, owned. He had restored and customised a Mini, which was painted lime green, had wide black arches, extra wide wheels, bucket seats and a racing wheel. Under the bonnet was a customised 1000cc engine. When I first laid eyes on it, it was love at first sight; I wanted it so bad. Mini cars were one of the most popular cars to be customised along with Ford Anglias and the newer Ford Escorts, which were used for racing each other on the local roads.

About six months later, my brother told me that Marco was thinking of selling his Mini. We went to meet Marco to discuss the deal and in a matter of ten minutes we shook hands on a price. All I had to do now was to find the money. I did not have a bank account, but I needed some cash and quick. After all, someone else might buy the car before I could raise the cash.

A few days later I was sitting in the manager's office at the local bank. I had just acquired another labouring job, which certainly helped. Some fifteen minutes later I walked out of the bank with the cash in hand. That night I was sitting in my very own car, one that was mine, one that I had dreamt so much of having, a car I had worked for and would continue to do so for some time. Never mind, it was mine. My ego was content; I was proud of my new possession and took great care of it. It was my new love, my life. But a few months later I noticed that my car was not so special any longer. It had the same colour, same sound, and handled the same way. It became familiar to me. Sure, I had experienced a race or two and the dangers involved. I had even lost a friend who had a fatal car crash whilst racing, but where had the magic gone? The reality was, that I still had a bank loan that needed paying. Fuel, insurance and tyres had to be paid for too, but where were the thrills?

Over the next year I released the idea of trying to be something I was not and would never be, another Jackie Stewart.[4] I sold the Mini, at a modest loss and decided to stay car-less for the near future. Now that I was looking into the past, I could see that those experiences were an important lesson for me, a step in the right direction to becoming ego-less.

Relu responded: *"We observed the risks you took when driving that car, the racing with others, trying to be the fastest, the best and at times some anger appeared. Do you know where that anger came from?"*

I reflected for a moment then replied: "Oh yes, I can clearly see it, it comes from a past life experience that has repeatedly reappeared in this life. I had been told by other mortals that I was not good enough, which has been a significant driving force for me to be the best and strongest. I believe I have worked a lot to transform this fear of not being good enough."

*"Yes, you have and the light you now hold is further confirmation of that. But you still have to be aware of your position in life and to be constantly vigilant*

---

4  Top British Formula One race driver of 1963-1973.

*against the return of the Ego's negative influences. The ego can reappear through others that may try to corrupt your feelings and thoughts. Do you have another experience you would like to revisit that may help explain your presence in the now?"*

Just as Relu finished speaking a strong beam of light filled my mind's eye and a door opened within it. Consciously I walked through the doorway into light and I found myself standing near a cliff's edge in the land of my physical birth; Wales. It was midday and I was walking in a circle to check an area of land that was being used by a dark group of the occultists. Witchcraft was present; I could sense and even taste it. But my clothes were different, more like the 1870's. I observed that during a meditation the previous night, I had been guided by a vision to come to this exact spot to clear the sacred ground of the negative energies. My actions would prevent the dark forces from abusing and using this original sacred place again. I could clearly see some of the markings that remained on the ground from previous satanic rituals. I continued to walk in a circle, taking an anti-clockwise direction. This would help release the old memories that were imbedded into the ground by the dark forces. Visions appeared in my mind's eye that revealed in greater detail what had taken place there with the coven of Black Witches. My higher guidance told me that they would visit this sacred ground every quarterly moon. I was shown several faces and given names of the leaders of the coven.

I continued the work to release all negative forces that the Master Witch had summoned. Then, out of the void I was creating, a disincarnate Black Witch moved into my space attempting to remove me. It set upon me and tried to permanently remove me from the sacred spot. It passed through my physical being causing me to flinch, but I remained strong and present in my light. I focused and projected light into the Black Witch, which immediately stepped back as the power and force of the light struck it. It tried to run and hide, but there was nowhere in the universe that it could hide. The dark force realised that I was holding it in a net of light and that its fate was imminent. Within the next few moments, I had transformed the darkness and returned it to its original place of light so that it might follow a true path of spirituality and reincarnate under divine law instead.

In those few moments of experiencing the powers of Black Witchcraft a whole new world opened for me, and from that moment on I would dedicate my life to serving the greater good. Exorcism was the means to transform any negative force that materialised preventing others from following their spiritual light path. I gradually returned to the present and I observed that Herali now stood behind my head, and Relu was standing at the bottom of my feet.

Relu asked: *"Do you now understand how your experiences of past lives as well as this life have elevated your consciousness towards even greater service to others?"*

"Oh yes, so that's why my clothes were so different. I had a past life experience."

Collectively the angels asked: *"Would you now like to return to the deeper experiences that await you on earth?"*

"I would, but what are they? Can you tell me?"

*"We cannot disclose what is to come for you; that would be breaking a Universal Law. Besides, what we say or instruct you to do may take you in a totally different direction to the one that your intuition might tell you. It is not for us to tell you which routes are the best to follow; you have been given the gift to decide and intuit what to do. It is important that you develop your natural intuition, let it be your guiding light."*

"But wait, what about the other question? Who am I?"

Relu responded: *"Spiritually speaking you are a Universal Child. On Earth you have had many names, some Shamanic like Kingfisher when you were a Native American Indian, others were more mortal. In this life span your parents named you Ralph because they thought it would suit your persona, your aura."*

"I agree. I have always liked my name."

*"Good, now the moment has arrived for you to embrace your reincarnation in accordance with the greater plan of Earth, which is for you to be fully realised. God speed, our beloved brother, we are but a thought away!"*

# Chapter 2

## Magical Life

I recalled that at some point early in the morning, I had developed a fever that lasted for most of the night, but now I felt more relaxed. I fell back into the timeless void and began to experience my transition from one world to another. Lights and colours were streaming past my periphery as I flew through the universe. I recognised the experience, but this was different; it felt as if I was passing through a channel of universal rebirth.

In the far, far distance I could see a tiny bright dot of light. A thought came to me. I recognised this galaxy and the constellation within it; that light is the Sun star. In a flash I was entering the Earth's atmosphere as my galactic trail of star dust disappeared behind me through the aura of earth. My very being, my soul was now emerging through the clouds as a familiar coastal region appeared miles below me. I felt hot, and then I was hovering over my physical body that lay motionless on the bed. I could see that the spirit within my physical body was intact. Me, my soul had been keeping all vital organs functional, which were connected to the universal umbilical cord.[5]

As I, my soul, re-entered the physical body, logic kicked into action and my physical senses awakened to my presence of being in a physical body. I was now

---

5  The stream of light that enters the Crown Chakra, which is only severed when physical death occurs.

looking out through two small holes called eyes. An immediate thought came to mind - what time is it? I deliberately paused for some moments to reflect upon the night that had passed. My whole body seemed to be really stiff as I reflected, hmm, that was a strong night. Fever, dreams and then more fever. But wait, is this me in the here and now? I feel different, lighter somehow. What happened?

I lay there trying to understand why I felt different this morning. I continued to take in the atmosphere; the sunlight that was flooding through the half-opened curtains, and a bird singing so joyously nearby. I rose to my feet and felt a bit shaky. I moved lightly towards the bedroom curtains that draped to the floor and fully opened them to be greeted by the delight of the morning light. The sunlight flooded in caressing and warming my whole body. I felt fresh, alive, even without showering.

What happened to me last night? In a flash I decided not to go to work; I wanted to be in nature today, to take a walk along my favourite hilltop, to feel the grass under my bare feet. With a single phone call, it was done. The secretary understood very well when I said I am not coming to work today. That was a positive step to take so early in the morning. What time was it anyway? It was 8 a.m. and I had overslept.

I stepped into the clinical like shower and turned the tap on. I could literally hear the melody of the falling water as it journeyed from the stream of the shower to caress my skin. The first drops of water impacted my skin. The water felt different too, it felt special and I wanted to feel the effects of the water running over my physical body forever. My skin felt even more alive as the water dipped in temperature. "What is going on today?", I wondered. I stepped back out of the shower,

grabbed a large fluffy towel and realised that my mother
was still using fabric softener against my wishes. This
time, it was apple blossom or something like that. A few
minutes later I had put on my hiking gear.

Breakfast was a simple matter of cheese and bread,
washed down by a cup of strong sweet tea. But even
the tea tasted different; I connected more deeply with
the tannin as it impacted my taste buds. During the
silence, eating my breakfast I was aware of the atmospheric pressure that filled the kitchen area. I opened
the patio doors letting in the natural fresh air that replaced the old. I stood there for a few moments watching the streams of light flooding through the broken
clouds that were passing over the valley below. Every
second or two the light changed as the elements of
sunlight and clouds created a dance. It was late spring,
and the garden was exploding with different shades of
green. Some spring flowers had already emerged, and
I sensed their perfume, even as the wind was blowing
the other way. That's strange; I never experienced that
before, what's going on?

I poured myself another cup of tea and went outside
and sat on the low patio stone wall. I observed the
nature that surrounded my home; seeing things I had
never really taken any notice of before. There hung a
broken branch on the oak tree standing some fifty yards
away. I wonder when that happened? There had been a
strong storm two weeks previously. Was it then?

I was alone in the house, my brother had got married
the year before and moved out, and my mother and
father were away holidaying in Spain. I intuitively felt
that this was a great time to be alone. Only three more
days left of work before my contract ran out. I reminded
myself that I had already felt that I would not be returning to my job. I did not like what I was doing, playing

with other people's money behind a cash counter, it was no longer fulfilling. Today I felt really positive that my direction in life was changing. No more trying to please others by selling them something they did not really want. My logic kicked in and whispered, look at you, you're at the ripe old age of thirty, you should have a regular job, a family, car and mortgage by now. What's wrong with you? An immediate reflection came back to me through another line of thought. Come on pick yourself up, there is nothing to regret, live for the moment, practice it, starting from now.

I was amused at my almost new line of thought: Yes, I must do more of that! Of course, I had had similar thoughts before. I recalled when I was five years old I had understood that all the animals on the farm lived in the moment, and that a dog will always come back to you with its tail wagging. Now that's, unconditional love.

I pushed my right foot hard into my bike boot, zipped up the back and reached across the corner of the Welsh dresser for my Belfast jacket and helmet hanging nearby. Some of the ornaments rattled as I nudged the dresser, reminding me of their fragility. I walked outside to the shed and straddled my classic blue Triumph Tiger Cub.[6] I reminded myself that the bike was made in the same year I was born. I never thought that a motorbike could be a Twin Soul, but it felt like it whenever I rode her. We were as one; pure pleasure. I positioned the kick start lever, turned the key, gave her a single kick and she started unceremoniuosly. We immediately headed for the hills, a short distance away, some fifteen minutes from the cottage.

The fresh spring air rushed past my face and the sunlight flickered through the new green foliage, as bike and I headed down the country lane. I arrived at the crossroads and stopped. I intuitively tuned into feeling

---

6  Triumph Tiger Cub is a 200cc British motor cycle. Manufactured in early 1953 – 1968.

which way to go. Logic suggested I go left towards the hills, but right followed the coast road that led to several beaches. My arms and whole body swung to the right. I pulled on the clutch lever with my left hand and clicked the gear lever down into first gear, opened the throttle, released the clutch from my grip and bike and I roared off towards a favourite beach. As we glided along, I felt good about the mechanics of my motorbike. It's a matter of synchronicity, I reflected; the spirit to ride and the mechanics doing the rest.

I wanted to be near to the sea for no special reason, but it felt right in that moment. I paused at another crossroads to get my bearings, then onwards. Some fifteen minutes later I arrived at Poppets beach. I pulled into the carpark and parked the bike. It was May, a quiet period for this predominately tourist area of Wales, and today was no exception; there were only three cars in the carpark. Leaving my helmet on the handlebar, I headed for the open beach, passing along one of the pathways that ran through high sand dunes.

To the right stood the National Lifeboat Station. Its' tourist gift shop was closed until the summer season. After fifty yards or so the dunes opened to a remarkable view of the open beach. I stopped for a moment to take it all in. I felt that everything was connected. The tide was completely out, but the golden sands were shimmering in the light all the way to the sea. As many times as I had visited this beach the nature that filled this estuary always astounded me, it was beautiful regardless of the seasons.

The river Teifi had forged its timeless way from the Cambrian Mountains to reach the Irish Sea, creating its renowned, peaceful beauty, and I was experiencing it now. There is a special light here, something that I had not really understood until this moment. The Irish Sea was calm, the waters rippled gently against the sand as each wave ended its journey. The light reflecting off the sea was like an effacement blanket upon the ocean that beautifully illustrated how these two elements are naturally connected, where sky and ocean become one.

I stood still for a moment longer to absorb the energy and take my bearings. To my right was the narrowed entrance to the estuary. To the left of the entrance were some yachts and few local fishing boats, which were moored behind a natural protective dune that had been strengthened to give shelter to a variety of boats. I observed that to the right of the river stood large sand dunes, behind which were three small roof-tops and chimneys. These were the local beach houses. Puffs of smoke were rising out of one chimney, giving it life, movement, a purpose. To my left in the far distance lay the rocky outcrop and cliffs that reached the water's edge. I decided to head for that area.

It was a beautiful view, and as I got closer to the cliffs a small farmhouse was just visible in the distance. It was not obvious at first, because it rested amongst the greenery of the new grass and foliage. There was an imposing mansion that stood near the edge of the cliff, and beneath it was an old lifeboat station that faced north, set back in a little bay. The station was protected by the cliffs and a stone pier that faced north. I remembered that the winds in this area were predominantly west-south-west. I reflected that this must have been a busy fishing port at one time. Pictures flooded my mind's eye as I imagined what it must have been like here a hundred or more years back, and how man must have been much closer to nature, almost by default, in those times.

Today was a great day. I stopped for a moment to take off my boots and socks. There was strength in the sun today, but the sand still felt cool beneath my feet and the puddles even colder as the ripples of water and sand pushed between my toes as I walked. I dipped my hand into the sea and tasted its salty residue, it felt alive and magically I was there to taste it.

My whole being was embracing the energy of the beach as I looked at the light that reflected off the sea, everything seemed to energise me. As I got closer to the rocky outcrop, I could hear the outgoing tide creating a musical melody unique unto itself. I noticed a figure sat on a rock. I realised it was Mark, a good friend of mine. I climbed the rock and we greeted each other with the usual warm embrace. He was wearing his favourite sandals and a heavy Afgan style shirt and jeans. His hair was down and was blowing gently across his face with the breeze.

"Fancy meeting you here", not pausing he continued, "I had an appointment today with the local newspaper that was cancelled. I decided to come here to help gather my thoughts about an art project that the local council is going to implement." He went on: "I intend to contest it on the grounds that it's environmentally unfriendly."

"Good for you," I replied, "standing for what you believe to be true."

There was a brief pause, then I continued: "I was just heading for the Carnigli hilltop but on reflection at the crossroads, I intuitively decided to come here instead. I love it when the intuition works; we are proof of that by us meeting today."

Mark looked knowingly into the sky and said: "Well there is always a meaning for everything. So why are we meeting today?"

I pondered on his question for a moment, and re-plied: "Does there have to be a reason? Maybe we were brought together just to be together. There doesn't have to be a reason, does there? I know that sitting here together and taking in the energy of this beautiful day is all there really is at this moment."

"You're probably right", he replied.

There was a long silence as we both contemplated on the synchronicity of our meeting. Two people were walking by beneath us. They too were carrying their shoes and socks as they walked through the shallow water. They looked up simultaneously and bid us "Good morning."

We both obliged with "Lovely day isn't it?"

"Oh yes", they replied. "it's here for the rest of the week."

They moved on smiling. In that moment I realised how simple it was to connect with total strangers through sharing something that brought joy to the heart, as nature does. Just seeing each other was enough.

I felt that Mark had picked up on my thoughts as he remarked: "Are you thinking what I am thinking?"

"I believe so." I felt like meditating too. "Shall we go over there to that large rock and meditate."

"That's interesting Ralph, it's where I usually sit to meditate when I come to this beach".

I felt good about listening to my inner thoughts. We positioned ourselves and together, entered our meditation. Immediately my senses became stronger, the smell of the sea, the sound of water gently washing over the rocks beneath us. Seagulls were communicating with one another as they flew above. The magnetic power of the rock was strong too. This was bliss. This, is why my intuition guided me to be here instead of in the office. Then I let go of the chit chat in my mind and entered a void where peace resided. I asked the universe to give me further guidance on my spiritual path. In an instant an outline of a being came to mind, one that I had seen on several occasions whilst meditating, but this time the light surrounding him was stronger.

Telepathically I asked "Who are you?"

The intuitive thought came back to me in a strong clear manner: "*I am your main guide Solomon. I am here to help guide you on your spiritual journey. I have been by your side from the first moment of your rebirth.*"

I briefly lost focus on the meditation and entered logical perception. I tried to get back to where I was in the meditation but was unable. I slowly opened my eyes and was flooded by physical light. I took a few deep breaths and waited for Mark to come out from his meditation. Some ten minutes later Mark returned from what I felt had been a strong deep meditation for him.

A few moments later, as he gathered himself, he said: "I like coming to meditate on this rock. It has a really strong connection to the universe; we must be sitting on a vortex."

"You're right", I replied. "I have met my main guide again, but this time it was different, it was stronger and clearer, for both of us I suppose."

"Don't doubt", said Mark. "Never doubt true spirit. It is us, the humans who are weak and corrupt, not spirits."

His words were powerful and timely, and rang true for me.

We sat there for an hour or more, sharing our experiences. I really felt that Mark was my spirit brother. I have a blood brother, and I love him too, but this was a different feeling I had for Mark. I said to him: "I feel that you are my spirit brother. I felt it the first time we met, must be some five years ago now, right?"

"You're right Ralph; I feel the same about you; time flies by when you're having fun."

We stood up and embraced each other, and in that moment a picture flashed past my mind's eye. I saw us as Native American Indians many lifetimes ago. I said to Mark: "We have been Native American Indians but from different tribes, this is our connection as spiritual brothers now, it's powerful isn't it?"

"Yes it is. Come on, let's go and have a cup of tea at my place,"

I replied: "You do like your tea Mark and I always thought I was a tea-oholic".

We both laughed and made our way down from the rock onto the sandy beach.

Mark lived in the village of Cilgerran that was near to where I lived. The village has a 13th century castle that was established by the Normans. In 1204 William Marshal, Earl of Pembroke, captured Cilgerran Castle from the Welsh, but just ten years later the castle was back in the hands of Prince Llywelyn. Today it still stands on a cliff above a gorge through which the river Teifi runs. The village is about three to four miles up-river from the beach.

Mark had lived alone for several years and I was beginning to understand why he liked his independence, which for me meant having the freedom to just be. His cottage lay down a lane just off the main street of the village. On arrival I duly parked my bike outside the front entrance of his cottage and waited for Mark to appear after he had parked his Morris 1000 along the main street. I had stayed with Mark many times before and in no time tea and toast were made. We sat outside at the back of his house on a small patio he had created.

The sun was just passing over the top of the roof and was bathing us in its warm spring light, just as it had all day. Like me, Mark was also a sun worshiper.

Our conversations always inspired me because whatever we talked about fed my spirit and soul, bathed in truth. We had our first cup of tea and I had already enjoyed two pieces of toast with some strawberry jam. I was about to spread some butter over my next piece, when Mark glanced across, his head slightly tilted and said: "Do you think the prime minister would mind us doing what we are doing, you know, not going to work, just sitting here sharing our thoughts in peace?" He continued in a slightly stronger manner: "Do you think that the country will grind to a halt because of this?"

In a flash I got his meaning, or at least my part in it and replied: "You're quite right Mark; I am absolutely sure that the country will continue very well without us. I do not feel guilty in any way about using my time to take care of myself."

A smile filled Marks face and a sparkle came to his eyes as we chuckled to ourselves.

Then he said: "Think of all those people who have not yet liberated themselves through spiritual practice. Following a spiritual practice does not mean that you must give up your daily job, become a vegetarian and stop drinking alcohol. It's a matter of what fulfils you and if you are being true to those feeling, that is the question for me."

I was already fully vegetarian. I had a beer or two on social occasions, but even the beer was disappearing quickly from my life. It did not taste good and the need for it was simply vanishing.

Over the next few hours we discussed the importance of purifying the body and mind, and how they interacted to create greater harmony or disharmony. I had come to understand that meat was a denser energy to vegetables;

it also held the fear of the animal before it was killed, as well as the chemicals that it was given, including antibiotics. So, for me, meat had become a no-no.

I was about to get up and leave when Mark said: "Hey Ralph, there is a Spiritual Church service at Newcastle Emlyn village hall tomorrow night. I'm going, would you like to join me?"

"Sounds good, what takes place during the service?"

"It's a bit Christianity orientated; but the main difference is that there is some spiritual philosophy, usually channelled and a medium will also lead a séance. There are also healing sessions taken at the end of the service."

"Sure, I would like that. What time does it start?"

"Oh, 7 p.m." said Mark.

"Great I'll see you there."

I raised myself off the sofa and bid Mark farewell with a brotherly embrace. I did not remember the journey home, as short as it was, I was so full of beautiful experiences, and my heart was exploding with joy. I felt my whole being was lighter as my inner voice told me "this is how life should be". I felt very poistive about following my inner guidance and was intrigued with what was to cross my path.

This was going to be my second experience of a spiritualist meeting; the first time was when I was sixteen years old. On that occasion my mother Regina had taken me. Regina was a Spiritualist church member and had attended many a Saturday service. She believed strongly in an afterlife, so here I was once more, with another opportunity to take part and make some new acquaintances.

It was becoming clearer to me that the Universal Law states that there is no such thing as chance. Whatever came into my life, gave opportunity in some form or other because there was greater wisdom behind it. I was curious. What was to come this night? What was I going to learn and experience? I was also aware of my expanding consciousness. By stepping out of controlling logic, it was beginning to dominate my reflections of future happenings.

On arriving at the location of the spiritualist gathering I realised that I had passed this small hall on a number of occasions. It stood alone at a junction in the upper part of Newcastle Emlyn, but I had never ventured within its walls. It seemed to be a lonely place. I recalled Marks words a few days ago: *"It was the village school in the nineteen forties and fifties"*.

I stood outside the entrance for a few minutes speculating. Surely there must be someone else in there by now? I took a deep breath and stepped forward to open what appeared to be the original door. I passed through the main door and was warmly greeted by an elderly woman whose energy field felt positive. She introduced herself as Ruth. She explained that she was the secretary of the Newcastle Emlyn Spiritualist Church, and that she was the chairperson for this evening's séance. I looked around the empty room, which I estimated could seat thirty to forty people. An elderly gentleman came through the main door and I duly moved towards a chair that felt right for me. As I sat down a young man and an elderly woman came in and were equally welcomed by Ruth.

The energy of the room felt good, but the air was musty from the scent of old furniture. Some seven or eight feet from the front row of chairs, stood a small reading table. It had a white linen cloth laid over it. On the right of the tabletop, there stood two glasses and a clear glass jug of water, a book, a candle stick holding a large candle, its flame flickering gently in the breeze.

Next to that, stood a small vase containing fresh flowers. Central, left of the room was a small, enclosed kitchen area from which a young man appeared. He was clean shaven, and smartly dressed in a light grey suit, white shirt, and a light pink tie. I thought perhaps he was the medium. Ruth turned around to greet him and beaconed him to be seated, gesturing with her right arm towards a chair. Just five minutes to go with but four of us gathered in the congregation. Apparently, it had started to rain heavily, as a group of four people came rushing into the hall shaking the rain drops off their clothes. I could hear the echo of the heavy rain falling on the rooftop. Another eight people appeared just as I checked the time on the old school clock on the wall. It was now a few minutes past 7 p.m. People were busily greeting each other as friends. Another couple entered and sat just behind me. One or two glanced my way and smiled, which was reassuring.

Ruth rose to her feet from behind the table to begin her introduction when Mark entered apologising with a slight bow and a smile for being late, and duly making his way towards me. He put his arm around my shoulder and greeted me.

"Good you could come Ralph", he said with a big smile on his face.

Ruth began by welcoming us all and continued by introducing the medium as Eric Jones, who resided in the city of Swansea. I was struck by the sincerity of the whole event. This included the mediums philosophical spiritually orientated view of life, the hymns that were sung and the séance itself. I felt it all blended well with the service. I was impressed at how clear and accurate the medium was in delivering the messages, both factually and with love.

As I tuned into his work a thought came to mind. I

wanted to become a medium too. The closing prayer was sung, and everyone was invited to stay for a cup of tea. Healing was also offered by a resident healer. Not one person left the room. I was struck by the fact that this was not only a sacred place of worship but also a social gathering, soul to soul. Spirituality was the essence of all that took place within the conversations I heard.

Mark introduced me to a couple; leaving me to get on with it. The atmosphere in the hall felt light with much joy; I was so happy to have been invited.

I noticed Ruth looking at me, and she returned my smile. I went to pour myself another cup of tea and she came and stood next to me, saying: "I hear you're a good friend of Mark."

"Yes" I said.

There was a pause, and then Ruth continued: "I'm starting a new meditation group this coming Friday. It's a closed group, you know, by invite only. I would very much like you to join us."

"Me? Are you sure?" I said.

"Why yes, I feel it will be very good for you."

I paused for a moment before answering: "I accept, and I'm most grateful."

"Excellent. Here is my address; we start at 19.00 sharp. See you then!"

We shook hands and she moved to the right to talk to another person. It then dawned on me that she had already written her address onto a piece of paper prior to our meeting. She knew I would come to the meditation evening.

Some moments later Mark came up to me and asked: "How's it going Ralph?"

"Many interesting things have been happening simultaneously", I replied as I glanced to my right. I noticed that two people had begun a healing session. The one receiving healing sat on a chair and the healer stood behind and simply laid their hands on the shoulders of the receiver. I could see how focused the healer was, and I was sure I could see a light energy around them.

Mark turned slightly to see what had attracted my attention. He quickly responded: "That's spiritual healing or laying on of hands, as it is often called. You know Jesus healed this way, so did Yoga Nanda a spiritual Guru from India who lived in America." Mark continued: "Mary is a very good healer too."

This form of healing was something that I also wanted to experience and I knew that the opportunity would come in the right moment. But in the meantime, Rodger said: "I hear that you are to attend Ruth's closed meditation group tomorrow night."

"Yes I am. This is just great. So many experiences in one place."

"That's how it is when you open the door to anything in life, there's so much more to see and embrace", said Mark.

Mary had finished the healing with an elderly gentleman, and I approached her and introduced myself to ask if I too could receive healing from her. She gave me a big smile and guided me with her right hand to sit on the chair. I gladly obliged. I tried to empty my mind of any expectations.

Then Mary said to me: "Relax as much as possible and clear your mind of any thoughts. Take a deep breath and let go of any tension you may feel in your physical body."

I tried to follow her guidance and in no time at all I felt that I was being elevated into another space. I no longer heard the people talking just a few yards away from us. A greater sense of peace now filled my whole being. I began to feel warmer, especially where Mary's hands were laid on my shoulders, but that warmth began to spread down my entire back and right leg. I saw flashes of light and colour, even a picture of a Native

American Indian's Tepee and some horses. Then I felt Mary retracting her hands and I gradually returned to logical consciousness. Mary had moved from behind and now stood in front of me as I opened my eyes. We then had a little chat about our experiences.

Mary said: "You have a lot of healing powers yourself; you're gifted, but are not yet using it."

I felt myself shrinking a little.

"It's okay you don't have to deny your gifts any longer, but you already know this from deep within yourself don't you?"

I nodded in agreement.

"You have a damaged right knee; a lot of energy went into healing that area, I could see that it had been twisted somehow."

"You're right, it's a Rugby injury that happened ten weeks ago, and it's still playing up a bit."

"It should improve now."

"I feel much calmer within, thank you so much. Can I give you a hug?"

We embraced and bid each other well. I realised that everyone else in the room had left apart from Mary, Eric, Mark and me. We all left the hall together and made our own individual ways home. I felt happy. This was a night to remember, no this was a week to remember, and it has not ended yet. There's the meditation tomorrow. night still to come.

I awoke the next morning with a call from the wild, the urge to be in nature. I knew an area where I wanted to be but had not yet ventured there to discover what magic it held. The weather remained good; still warm and sunny. An hour later I was heading for a National Reserve area, an oak forest that was reputed to be over two thousand years old. On arrival I parked my bike and headed for an open field that lay before the ancient forest. Historically this whole area was once covered in oak, which was used to build the traditional Welsh cottages and ships, such as Schooners, used to transport goods such as coal, from one port to another, along this stretch of coastline.

I reached the edge of the field and hopped over the fence to enter the small oak forest. The atmosphere was alive with the perfume of spring, and the energy of the greenery bathed my eyes and blended with my body, as a gentle breeze caressed my face. The weather had been exceptionally mild this year and spring had indeed come early. The oak in this part of the country tended to be smaller, which I felt was partly due to the strength of wind that generated along this valley.

I was now walking through an ocean of Bluebells, trying not to step on any. The eminence of a bountiful spring was all about me, and wild garlic shoots were appearing. "How magical nature is", I thought to myself. I had heard local superstition was that Merlin the Wizard had a cave in this very wood. 'Would I find it today?' I stood for a moment to absorb the energy, natures perfume, the light and the sounds of birds rejoicing. I could see the Caterpillars munching away at the new leafy shoots of oak and the silvery spider's webs that spanned space, connecting one plant to another. My heart was full of joy, it mattered not if I ever found Merlin's cave. I was here now to experience something similar. It was my experience, just as Merlin's must have felt during his timeline here, on earth.

I took off my shoes and socks to truly connect with Mother Earth. After some time, I entered a natural clearing, in the middle of which stood a small mound of earth and rocks. How interesting it looked. It was about twenty feet high and twice as wide. I made my way over to the mound and stood at the bottom, pausing for a moment. In seconds, a cold chill ran down my entire back. I felt that this place was indeed special. Maybe it had been a place of worship in past times. Not far from here stood a Megalithic burial chamber dating back to approximately 3500 BC. Was there a connection between these two places?

I climbed the small mound to find it had a bowl like quality. Some large rocks formed what seemed to be a broken circle. I closed my eyes for a moment to go deeper into feeling the energy of where I stood. I calmly removed my clothes. I stood there, naked, as the day that I was born. I raised my arms and turned to face the sunlight that was streaming through the foliage of oak leaves. I thanked God for my life, for the experience of this moment. I thanked God for the family I had and for my family of friends too. I had never felt as complete as I felt in those moments.

I then realised that I was not of this earth. I had awakened to another me, but what was I doing here, and what was my deeper calling? I was now just beginning to discover some of the magical life experiences. How long I stood there I do not know, nor did it matter. I lay down on a bed of grass and moss as the smell of earth filled my being. I was locked into the present moment of BEING as in the spirit of earth and the surrounding nature engulfed me. I drifted off into a sleepless sleep, a place where no other could go. There was no need to escape, run or hide; after all, I was just BEING.

I was awoken by the sound of a fox calling. The sun had passed by and it felt much cooler. It must be late afternoon. I looked up towards the sun and estimated it was about 3.30 p.m. I sat up and stretched my arms and legs, then cuddled up into a ball (as if in the womb of nature) for a few moments more. I suddenly realised the meditation was tonight and I should not be late for my first group calling. I dressed with a sense of urgency

and then blessed the sacred place and made my way
back to my beloved Triumph and home.

# Chapter 3

## Light Body

It was fast approaching 6 p.m. and only an hour to go until the meditation. I had prepared my physical self; showered and shaved, feeling the excitement growing within me. I felt like I needed to wear some light-coloured clothes tonight. For years I had consciously or unconsciously chosen to wear dark or black clothes. A complete turnaround was taking place here too; white was now in, black and grey out, I thought to myself as I rustled through my wardrobe. This felt good; outer as well as inner change was taking place. I recalled what Mark had said to me in the Spiritualist church: "*What you look like on the outside reflects what you feel on the inside.*" Which on reflection was a fair comment at the time, but now I was experiencing this strong change as a reality.

Directly in front of me hung a single pair of beige trousers and a white shirt, one that I had worn to a funeral a year back. I grabbed them. This would have to do, but I would get some new clothes soon. It had come to my mind some months back that if I wore white as well as brighter coloured clothes it would help harmonise my body vibration.

Time was moving on. I hated being late for any occasion. I looked at the bedside clock; it was 6.30 p.m., and then rushed to the bathroom. In a matter of minutes, I was on my way.

I parked my Triumph on the main road in front of the Newcastle Emlyn post office. I glanced at the village clock on the tower of the old courthouse. It was 6.53 p.m. I looked at the address that Ruth had given me, and yes this was the street, but which side was I on, odds or evens? I turned and faced a door that had number 16 on it; good it must be close by. I walked along to numbers 20, 22 and ah, there was 24. I approached the partly opened wooden door, rang the bell and someone shouted: "Come on up Ralph."

I entered and climbed the stairs which led to a top floor flat. Ruth appeared at the top of the stairs to greet me saying: "'You can hang your jacket on the coat hanger behind you, would you like a cup of tea?"

"Oh yes, please."

I duly hung my coat on the already overflowing coat hanger.

On entering the living room, I noticed that there were eight of us in all. Mark came over to say hi, and commented: "You're looking a bit different Ralph. You're shining a bit more tonight."

I thanked him for his observation and confirmed to him that I actually did feel lighter, not weight wise but spiritually. Chairs were already laid out in a circular formation. On a table behind the circle, stood some glasses of water, and I helped myself to one. I had realised that spiritual activity such as meditation, for some reason, made me thirsty. I had noticed the previous night when Eric was giving the séance, he drank a lot of water too. I wondered if it helped the energy flow well.

Everyone was sat on their chosen chairs. Mark sat opposite to me to help balance the energies as we were the only males in the group. To my right was Kim and to my left was Sandy; we had already introduced ourselves.

Ruth cleared her throat and began to speak in a strong clear manner, which I liked.

"This is a new group for creative visualisation meditation, and I can already see that you are quite developed in your mediumship and spirituality, which is why you are here."

I understood that she was reading everyone's energies; she could see our Chakras and Aura's. I did not feel threatened by this in the least; in fact, I quite liked the idea. It demonstrated to me that Ruth was a true clairvoyant; she knew what she was doing. I felt in good hands here.

"There is no time set for how long this group will continue to meet. It will follow its own course and the end will come when it is right."

I felt good about that, just trusting the universe to allow the flow to occur.

Ruth continued: "I would like each of you to introduce yourself, starting clockwise and to my right is?"

"Hello, I am Mark."

There was a brief pause as Mark cleared his throat and continued his introduction by sharing some experiences and insight of his personal spiritual journey. This was followed by Gwyneth, then Kim, me, Sandy, Megan and Rhyan.

"Good", Ruth said, when Rhyan had ended her personal introduction. "Now because you are already prepared individually for tonight's meditation, I would like you to seek guidance from the other side[7] that is connected to someone in the group. First seek to connect to your main guide.[8] Your guide will help you on this journey, or you can simply ask the universe for guidance, remember all spirit forms can read the

---

7   Meaning another realm in another constellation, as in heaven and earth.

8   Every individual has a main spiritual guide from their birth. The guide remains connected to assist the individual's spiritual growth when they have begun to awaken to spiritual realities.

thoughts that are passing through your mind. Spirit will oblige you with their guidance if it serves the greater good. There is no set time for this meditation, you can open your eyes when your meditation has finished, but remain silent and hold the energy, as others may still be deep in their meditation. Does anyone have any questions?"

I asked: "Are you going to guide us a little bit?"

"Oh yes Ralph, I forgot, thank you for reminding me. I will guide you at the beginning of the meditation, to be more relaxed, where you can let go of your physical self in order to enter your higher consciousness. From there on it's your journey. Good let's begin. I will be with each of you throughout the meditation because it is my place to hold the energy. I am a bit like a shepherd caring for its flock."

I noticed that the clock on the wall behind Ruth read 19.35; time had indeed been transformed since I first walked through the door.

She began guiding us to relax more deeply by using the breath, which helped me to be more deeply connected to my own rhythm. Then she instructed: "Remember to ask spirit for guidance in order to receive guidance, your now in a school of meditation."

It certainly felt like that, and I trusted Ruth 100%.

As she guided us though the initial steps of the meditation thoughts came and went, as did the picture like images. I felt the vibration of the circle to be strong, and for a moment I peeped with my right eye to see if everyone else had their eyes closed. They did. I recognised that I was a bit insecure and began to focus more deeply on my meditation technique. I quickly found myself drifting away into a void. I intuitively asked spirit for help, which was immediate and went even deeper into the void. I then found myself to be flying in an aeroplane that was noisy and shaking. To my left sat another passenger who was calmly reading a newspaper and seemed to be oblivious of the shuddering of the plane. I glanced at the newspaper and next to the title was the date 18th September, 1979. I then began to have the sensation that my physical body was levitating, it felt so light, I was sure that I was hovering some two or more feet above my chair in the room where I was meditating. It was the strangest feeling I had ever had. I managed to stay focused on what I was experiencing and continued.

I was sitting in an iridescent light, and next to me sat a woman who introduced herself as Anwen. She knew I had heard her thoughts and smiled back at me. It seemed as if she could see me for real.

She then said: *"Tell my beloved sister that this is what happened to me, but I am alright now. I am at peace, we are amongst others who share their peace, with like minds, we are with God. Please ask my sister not to mourn for me any longer. It is time for her to rest as well and to let go of me."*

I felt her sincerity, her love and the warmth of her smile filled my very being.

The plane then started to shudder and rock more violently. A lightening flash appeared in my mind's eye and the plane took a dive. As the aeroplane plummeted, everyone on board was screaming, luggage flew through the air and people were falling over each other like cards. Then there was silence, a silence deeper than I had ever experienced before. Everything became calm, like the ocean after a storm had passed into nothingness. I was being carried off in a wave of light, and in the next moment I could feel my soul-self re-entering my physical body. I landed with a thump. My entire body shook and I opened my eyes quickly to see that Ruth had been watching me.

"Are you alright Ralph?" she asked.

I sat in silence for a moment to gather my senses.

"Take a sip of water my beloved, it will help ground your energies. I can see that you've been far away!"

I followed her advice and felt that everyone else in the room had been waiting for my return, but they were smiling and I understood that they were happy for me.

After a long silence Ruth asked the group if anyone would like to share any message that is connected to someone in the room. There were some moments of silence before Rhyan hesitently raised her hand.

"Please go ahead Rhyan", said Ruth.

"Well, I'm not sure who this is for, but I feel it's for you Gwen."

Gwen responded immediately by sitting up straight in her chair.

"Okay I'm listening." said Gwen.

"A small baby came to me; it was not yet born. It was a boy who told me that there were some complications during the pregnancy, your pregnancy. The child aborted by itself because the union between you and your then partner had changed dramatically when you became pregnant. The baby told me that you were not to blame for the miscarriage. Shortly after, your partner left you and you were alone again. He had deserted you before, but you were not ready to accept how things were then, but now you can."

I felt the energy in the room sinking. This was very personal stuff here. Was it ok to give such a message? I could see that Gwen was struggling to hold her composure and eventually started to sob. I also felt the compelling drive of Rhyan to get the entire message out and she continued: "The soul of the child told me to pass the message to you, for you to understand that what happened was an instrument to help you wake up to the fact that your partner was negative to you most of the time, he was not true to himself and could not be true to you either. This was the meaning of my coming to you tonight; to help you realise that you can find true love."

Now Gwen was really crying, but everyone sat in their chairs holding the energy of the circle, which was now stronger and even lighter.

There was a long pause before Gwen responded: "Thank you Rhyan for sharing your message with me. I now understand how wise the universe is and how death can also heal. I take this to my heart and will listen to the advice given."

A longer pause ensued before Ruth spoke in a softer voice: "Everyone here is a messenger for spirit. What may seem difficult to accept at first can be a strong healing, when it is seen in the light of truth, that is, not personal."

There was a moment's pause and she continued: "Right, who would like to share next?"

Mark and Megan gave their messages, which were also deeply compelling. Then I felt that I must release what I had experienced some thirty minutes ago. I waited for the moment and then said: "I would like to share now."

"Fine", said Ruth, "Take your time Ralph."

"Well, I am also not sure who this message is for, but my instincts tell me it's for you Kim."

Kim said: "Thank you Ralph, I am curious, please tell me what you have from spirit."

I took a deep breath to help centre myself and felt calm and collected. I then reconnected to the channel of Anwen and began to relive the experience, explaining it exactly as it was in my vision from the spirit world. Whilst I was presenting my insights to Kim she occasionally nodded her head in confirmation. I reached the end of the message and everything went blank. Again

I felt that I was returning to my physical body, but this time it was a lighter experience.

Kim said with emotion: "Thank you, Ralph."

She confirmed that what I had said was true, and she continued: "In September 1979 my sister Regina was returning from America just after getting married to a Spanish American. They were flying over the Atlantic on their way back to Stansted airport, and eventually on to Wales, when the aircraft was lost over the ocean. No wreckage was ever found or recovered, no bodies, nothing! I thank you so much for this insight Ralph; my heart can now rest knowing that she is at peace on the other side."

It was a wonderful feeling to have confirmation that what I had experienced was true, and it had helped to heal both worlds. I then completely understood that I had a light body, another aspect of me, that could be anywhere in the universe whilst the physical aspect of me was grounded and safe. I also now understood that other spirit beings could see and interact with me whilst I was on earth. I found this fantastic but still surreal.

Everyone had relayed their messages and was now sharing their experiences over a cup of tea before leaving. Ruth had explained that we were to meet every week, same time, same place. Everyone seemed pleased with the evening's events and Mark expressed his gratitude for my attending. I was grateful too. I went to gather my things to leave when Kim came over to me and gave me a strong hug.

"Thank you, Ralph, that was such a help. All these years I have been in the dark, not knowing, but now it is all so clear, you are indeed a light worker."

I thanked her and explained that I now understood that I was simply being used by Spirit as a messenger, a way of connecting disincarnated spirits to incarnated spirit beings, as in you or I.

Kim agreed and Mark, who was standing nearby, confirmed as well.

"That is so true, and may it continue to grow."

The three of us chuckled and smiled at each other.

# Chapter 4

## Staying Grounded

Over the next six months I had many spiritual experiences. I gave hands on healing after attending another spiritualist meeting at Newcastle Emlyn. John, who I had met once previously, approached me after a service and asked if I could give him healing, so I gladly obliged. I was avidly reading three esoteric books simultaneously. I could not get enough of the occult; my appetite for spiritual knowledge and the wisdom it gave was insatiable.

Some of the people with whom I had grown up were telling me how I had changed since I started being more spiritually orientated. It was true, I started to reject alcohol, and I became a full vegetarian, no fish or meat. I no longer judged others. Gossiping was out, as was small talk. It no longer interested me; a waste of space, as I felt that my time, and how I spent it had become precious. I was seeking conversations that fed my soul and awoke my spirit, not my ego. My appetite for life had changed for the better as far as I was concerned.

Some of my friends tried to entice me to join them at one or two parties, which I gladly attended without consuming alcohol. Some could not understand how I could enjoy myself at a party without getting drunk. It seemed to me that alcohol was a necessary ingredient for others to socialise. I felt this was no longer my way. I needed to be clearheaded and present, to feel more deeply what was taking place in my immediate environment. As I stood there amongst the dedicated drinkers it became clear how I had used alcohol to help release the stress I was carrying. I now realised that the effects of alcohol blocked and numbed my emotions and responses. I recalled when I would fall out with my girlfriend, how I'd head for the pub to either drown my sorrows or open my emotions to another that was willing to listen to my complaints and judgments.

I was now following another path. I wanted solutions and clear answers to the meaning of life. I no longer wanted to be confused by my emotions through which the ego was continually trying to control my spiritual body. I was seeking deeper insights into what energy is, and how it was flowing through what I now recognised to be my temple, my physical body. Esoteric science, quantum mechanics and physics became three of my favourite topics of study, but I was very keen to understand the alchemy of life and its mysteries.

Previously I had believed that science and spirituality were one, but now I understood that I had missed an important fact. The study of science is chiefly left brain orientated, which is the mechanical side where proof is required, which is very black or white. It is limited to the physical dimension and tells us how things work, which is perfectly fine and has greatly advanced how we live on one level. But for me spirituality was now giving me another perspective of how to live, as my higher senses were now opening and expanding.

In a matter of a few months, I had dropped many of my normal routines that had been based on the needs of logical consciousness. I was going deep into studying my own expectations and judgments. I certainly felt different within but was it enough? I wanted to be "enlightened". I had read many books regarding enlightenment, but none seemed to address the basic question of how to obtain enlightenment, other than seeking council from a spiritual teacher, who were often referred to as gurus. I lived so far away from India and its rich spiritual philosophy, so who was there to trust? I had a few spiritually minded friends such as Mark, who I saw as my spirit brother, and, also Ruth, who ran the meditation group. I was a mere mortal, as were those who were amongst my new social group of spiritually minded people. It became more apparent that everyone had their own imbalances to deal with, including me. I knew that I was far from being clear of the ego's ambitions to control the logical aspect of mind, emotion and feelings. I desperately wanted to change.

It was a sunny Tuesday morning, and I was sitting at one of my favourite spots on a riverbank along the river Aeron. I was thinking that there must be ways to become enlightened, other than following a guru. Books were fine for teaching mental spirituality but being intellectually spiritual was not for me, it had to come from the heart with a clear conscience.

The wise words that Mark spoke many months back on the beach flooded to into my mind: *"I find it difficult to trust any human being because the ego can corrupt their consciousness and their true intent. The only thing I trust 100% is Spirit, Spirit are of the light, nothing is hidden, and the guidance I receive from my main guide has always been true."*

This, I felt, was an important key that would help open doors for my own spiritual development. I will create a stronger contact with my main guide so that I may receive universal wisdom with insight. This is how I will liberate my logic and expand my consciousness by opening the door into the right hemisphere of the brain. I stretched myself over the grass and immediately felt deeply connected to heaven and earth. I drifted off into a timeless sleep.

I was awoken by a few drops of rain falling upon my face. A few more raindrops fell as I rose to my feet, it was a short shower that was over in seconds, but the wind was picking up from a southerly direction. Time to move. As I walked, I felt a bit strange; my body did not feel so connected to the ground. I felt lighter, indeed much lighter. I stopped for a moment to observe where I was. I was walking through an open meadow that was awash with daisies and dandelions. It felt good, very good but I was not fully connected to my physical senses. The trees were not separated from the grass; neither was the flowing stream of the river from the stones that it passed over. The now blue sky had a few white clouds that were passing by; everything was connected, as were the trees with earth and sky, the river with the land. I felt timeless, as if I were in a vacuum but all was well in my life.

I walked on in a state of bliss, wondering if this was Nirvana. I continued holding my state of consciousness, for how long, I could not tell, but I gradually re-entered the logical perception of life and the physical senses reconnected. I stopped for a moment and sat down on a large log that had been abandoned by the last flood water, where I contemplated my state of being.

I caught sight of a small ant hill, and the ant colony were busy doing their thing. For a few moments I became an ant and was looking up at myself, too big to comprehend. Was God looking down on me in this moment just as I was looking at the ants. I was busy going about my life, but what was I trying to build, what was my instinctual self, telling me?

Three months had passed since I had the insight by the river. Today I felt that I was losing touch with my spirituality, it no longer seemed fun. I realised that I had become too serious, too mentally orientated. My development to expand my consciousness to be fourth and fifth dimensionally orientated, and to reach the horizon of life, that of higher consciousness activity, began to feel like a weight on my shoulders. I found myself analysing myself and spent far too much time operating outside of my physical senses that help ground the human body. Higher consciousness activity was now dominating my life.

For the last five weeks I had been focused on training my intuition. I wanted to feel and know what was to come into my life a week ahead. Then I graduated to feeling what was to come in the next day. I knew who I would meet tomorrow. I became so finely tuned into universal activity that I could tell what would happen in the next moment. I felt lost in the knowing, where were the adventures in life, the mystery of what the future may bring? Suddenly, not knowing seemed much more attractive than knowing. The activity of experiencing future happenings raised a number of questions. Is everything pre-planned? Was this a holographic experience? Had everything already happened? Was I living in a virtual world?

I felt that I was going crazy, I was losing it, my faculties, and my general feeling of wellbeing were diminishing. Everything began to feel very heavy. A great depression came over me in a matter of hours. I felt psychically blocked through my own psychic actions. I felt that I had over stretched what I now understand to be my limited abilities to process and harmonise the higher vibrations of light that I had opened myself to. The left and right hemispheres of mind, my consciousness, had once blended and been in harmony. But now there was a distinct lack of harmony, the higher octave that had not so long ago, dominated my mental abilities to process basic physical actions, was gone. I felt terribly weak on all levels; my spiritual world was crashing. Everything that I knew and practiced in relation to my spiritual journey no longer mattered to me. I could not meditate or even consider it. I could no longer read any books associated with spirituality. I had heard of the word zombie, but until now had paid little attention to its true meaning; now I felt *zombiefied*. I was numb to my own feelings and others around me. I was not present, and others noticed that I was not my usual cheerful self, the positive one, the one who gave advice to others when asked. Where was I? Who was I? What had I become?

Five weeks had past and I was still in the doldrums, locked away in self-pity and remaining in a general state of negativity. I had dug myself into a hole. I decided this had to change and I began to focus on changing things. It came to me that I needed go into seclusion. Within the first week of my self-imposed solitude, the cloud that I had created in my aura and consciousness, became heavier. I was not paying enough attention to being present. I became lost in mind games. Meanwhile, Ruth contacted me and invited me to do some mediumship work at the Newcastle Emlyn Spiritualist Church at the end of the month. The phone started to ring with people wanting healing. I even got an inquiry to help heal a horse. I said no to all of them.

My lack of interest not only in spirituality but life itself became overwhelming. I felt like I was dying from within. My heart was beating but I did not feel alive. The fire within had diminished; I was no longer feeding it. I was no longer interacted with nature either, which had been such a big part of my life. I found it difficult to still my mind.

During a moment of contemplation, it occurred to

me that I could use logical perception to help lift me out of my depression. But how? I began to apply logical reasoning to examine and access the past experiences of my waking up to spirituality. I began to analyse the pros and cons of the choices and actions I had taken, which gave me valuable insight into cause and effect.

I began to write a list of my judgments and placed them into categories of right or wrong, which opened my eyes to how my ego had gained control over me. Gradually over the coming months I felt that I was beginning to narrow the gap between logic that was aligned with ego (the unconscious) and intuition; crossing the bridge as it were. I felt that there was a subtle shift in consciousness taking place between all my senses.

I was developing the ability to switch on or off my three higher senses, to use them only when required to help others. This was, itself, a dramatic change. Previously I had been reading almost everyone's aura, even reading their mind, their inner thoughts. People would often give me strange looks when I applied my consciousness in this manner. I now understood that this behaviour, as innocent as it was, was in fact an intrusion into their sacred space, a violation of their consciousness. Yes, telepathy does work, but I should take greater responsibility as to how I applied it. Curiosity alone was not the right motive; integrity had to be right up there in tandem. Every thought should be spiritually based, which required grounding, otherwise my thoughts and actions would not be fruitful.

I also took a long hard look at my ego self and clearly saw how the ego was always looking outside of itself by judging others and was unwilling to take responsibility for its actions. In this manner, society had also conditioned me to think and behave egotistically. Fear is a factor of ego trying to control my choices. If ego's criteria were not fully met, then look out, judgment day. Oh it's your fault, you did this to me because of ... My ego was always hungry for attention, to be in control, even to the degree of not allowing others to share their truth.

Another positive aspect appeared when I recognised that the three bodies of energies, the physical, spirit and soul were not separate but a part of one unified force. I knew that the key to enlightenment was to harmonise these three bodies of energy to become one. In my haste to develop spiritually I had chiefly ignored my physical presence which removed the grounding for the spirit and soul. Without correct polarisation of the three forces, it was not possible to transform the shadow self, and the ego would remain locked into my physical dimension. The polarisation and flow of Kundalini[9] was being limited and certain chakras could not be liberated by the burning away of any negative energies held. If I did not apply correct consciousness, the flow of kunda-lini would continue to be blocked and the lack of free play between the chakras would remain.

I began more earnestly to apply a positive frame of mind into whatever I did, with the understanding that gradually the flow of energy would increase throughout my entire physical body. Any positive thought I had, increased and strengthened my polarity, which effectively helped increase the flow of blood through a positively charged central nervous system.

Some three months later I was beginning to feel much stronger in all three areas of body, spirit, and soul. It became clear that a positive flow of energy and its blending with my energies, was chiefly down to the state of mind that remained free of any ego control and emotional disturbances.

---

9   Kundalini is a light frequency that holds three fires, which are the fire of friction, fire of electric and the atomic fire. These forces between them pass downwards and upwards through all seven Chakra centres in a continuous flow, lifting and transforming any impurities that remain within the vibration of each Chakra.

It was late afternoon as I sat in a deckchair in the garden of my parent's house. The sun was disappearing behind some dark clouds; I could tell that a low weather front was upon us. It suddenly became chillier followed by a steady stream of cool air. These were classic signs of rain. I stayed put and closed my eyes. I had no specific question, but in that moment, I just felt like meditating. The light of the day faded, and it became cooler. An insight came to me. Conscious thought is a spark of light that must go somewhere, so how I direct my thoughts, creates whatever I receive. I held the energy for a moment and questioned myself to check whether I was being purely logical about such a thought. I went deeper and followed my inner dialogue.

Logical thought patterns are chiefly created by conditioning, the way I was brought up, at home, in school and in society. Thought is consciousness and what I do with it helps create whatever it is directed towards. It may not be physical at that point but it is still energy in motion and will follow universal laws, which manifests itself, in some form, to wherever it is directed. I understood that the one receiving my thought may then pick up the phone and say *"I just felt like calling you, I don't know why, I just felt like it"*. Bingo!

On a subtle level the action and reaction were flowing in a positive way, which must also be true for the negative. I realised I had to take much greater care of my thoughts, to hold them, to be aware of when or how I project them into the field of universal consciousness. For me, this was the matrix into which every soul is connected; God consciousness. Another thought came flooding in. Spirit knows exactly what I am thinking as well as what I am feeling, because thoughts tranforms into feelings. Sometimes it can be the other way around, but the feeling might be related to a thought that someone is sending you. So, there are different forms of thought or feeling, but essentially it's about awareness. Being sensitive to my environment, recognising which are my energies or not and what to do with them, is important to develop. That's it. I needed to be more focused on being tuned into my feelings and thought, and then they would complement each other.

# Chapter 5

## Logical Stability

### A Step towards Enlightenment

Whilst studying my thoughts for a whole day I realised how often I slipped into memories of the past and future worries or fears. I realised it would require a stronger conscious effort on my behalf to remain fully present. It was interesting because I did not consciously realise that I was, 85% of the time, either in the past or the future, unless I logically paid attention to it. This brought up two questions. The first, was how did being present connect to becoming enlightened? I knew that the past, present and future are physical laws that give a physical dimension to the structure of life. They help demonstrate the value of being present. If I was not focused on the present moment, then where was I? The past is history; I cannot live there or be in it. It is not true reality, so why do I find myself wishing to be there so often? The future has not yet come, so why am I so worried about it? Memories and experiences are important in respect of giving guidelines that help us choose what to do next. But that is only true if I remain there for a short period of time. If my mental approach to life is transfixed on the past, I will be lost in it, continually reliving it, whilst on the other hand if my mind is overstimulated towards future happenings then I am equally lost. The future has not yet come, so why waste so much time and energy on futuristic speculations?

I began to realise more deeply the wisdom of being present and was now seeking positive solutions to change my way of being. I meditated on this very question down by the river, and centred myself to a point of deep stillness. As I went deeper into the meditation, a stream of tinted blue light flooded my consciousness and through it walked my main guide Solomon. He stood majestically before me and our telepathic communications began ...

"I have felt you close to me for many months now. Was it you who has been guiding me during my times of contemplation and meditation?"

*"Yes it was me, and as I have said before, I am ready to serve."*

"Are you, um, how shall I put this? Are you the king Solomon of old, you know the one in the history books and the Old Testament?"

*"Yes, I am."*

"Wow! I really feel honoured."

*"I respect your feelings, but that was then, and this is now, no ego, remember?"*

"I am deeply touched by your presence and I will try to do my best to follow your guidance."

*"The first lesson is that it's not a matter of trying, it's about BEING."*

"You're absolutely right. I will work hard on BEING."

Solomon then immediately said: "*You have been having some interesting insights over the last few days, and you are correct in understanding that whenever you are operating through the physical timeline of 3D consciousness, your actions and the reactions are controlled by physical laws. This is where fear and ego can come into play; because the ego cannot be present for more than a second in the present, and will try to take your thoughts into either the past or future in an effort to control your psyche.*"

There was a long pause.

"Please continue."

"*The ego is not of the light, it is not a manifestation of God, which is why it always seeks to be in control. One of the ego's main agendas is to control you through fear, which is why you have been spending much of your life living in the past or future and seldom the present.*"

"So it comes back to that again, the ego?"

"*You read my mind. If you did not fear, past or future would not be in your consciousness, you simply would BE. This is the lesson that many are learning on earth at this critical time, how to BE by BEING!*"

"But won't I miss out on life, the experiences of physical life, to taste food, to swim in the oceans and to hear the birds singing?"

"*Quite the opposite, you will be deeply in touch with life because you are experiencing life through the eight senses, not five. You will be experiencing the fullness of life through the spirit and soul meaning of life. You will interact and blend with others more profoundly because you will not judge and are not being controlled by the ego. Your soul will guide your every thought and action, without fear, no ego. When you are being present there will be peace within your whole being because nothing else can be there but love, light and joy!"*

"Oh, I've been living a lie then, not true to myself or others. Is this the illusion so many write and talk about?"

*"Don't be so hard on yourself. You have come a long way since you first decided to come to earth from your own constellation. Earth is a strong place to develop spiritually and what you learn will not be wasted. You and many like you are of great value to earth because you carry light into the dark areas in order to transform the evil and ego; it's the most natural thing you can do."*

"Now I really feel the pressure to become enlightened."

*"You are already that, but you are not yet fully re-alised. Let me put it another way. The density of your physical consciousness or logic, does not hold the experiences you have already had; those are in a higher vibration of light where they cannot be cor-rupted, which is why you cannot recall a past life unless it is given through meditation and the activ-ity of higher consciousness. For many a lifetime you have been experiencing what it's like to have an ego, which has been a fertile ground for your spiritual growth. Through those experiences you have initi-ated to your present point of your spiritual develop-*

*ment, which is why you are now about to initiate into a deeper healing school to help others who are not so aware."*

For a second I heard the melody of the river flowing by and then went back into meditating. I looked at my fears; it became clearer that fear was the underlying energy that often motivated me to become lost in both the past and future. If I were not able to trust myself how could I trust another? To fear the loss of anything was embedded in my logic, and to a great degree I had been programmed and conditioned to behave in this manner by social structures. I could now see the cycle that prevented me from being present, due to the illusions that fear creates.

Solomon then spoke again: *"You now have clear insight into what is; now it's a matter of applying what you have learnt into everyday activity."*

"Being present is the only place where I could be self-realised, no fear and without ego, which is what being present is. There is only that moment, that is all there ever is, the true reality of being present."

*"Yes, you have the general idea. When in the now there is so much going on but yet, nothing is happening. I am neither alive nor dead. I am all things, yet nothing."*

As I took the next breath, there was but a moment to activate my thoughts in a correct manner. I was seeking to motivate my spirit to move my body so that I could fully interact with the life experience. wasn't that beautiful? I will set myself some targets to follow, and I began to mentally record them:

- For the first day check my thoughts every 30 minutes.
- For the second day check my thoughts every 45 minutes.
- For the third day check my thoughts every hour.
- For the fourth day check my thoughts every two hours.
- For the fifth day check my thoughts every three hours.
- For the sixth day check my thoughts every four hours.
- For the seventh day check my thoughts four times a day.

"I believe I have it all worked out now, I will learn so much more about myself through applying this practical method."

*"That looks good. Remember, I am but a thought away."*

With reverence I thanked Solomon for his assistance and slowly came out of my meditation, physically reconnecting to earth. I felt my life force to be extremely sensory, everything was connected and alive with the force, which I had come to understand as LIGHT.

For the first two days I tried to observe and experience my checkout list, and at first, regularly forgot to have a mind check on being present. But by day three the self-observation began to notice when I should have a reality check. On day four I pretty much followed the course I had set.

As day five flowed I even caught myself taking another reality check in between the hours prescribed. Day six was a mixture of day two and three. Day seven was simply remaining focused on being present, and for an hour or two I managed to be fully present.

Whenever I was fully present it reminded me of when I had been playing with children. They made being present easy. How many times had I fully loved a person whilst being with them? Was it for a second or two, a minute or more, or was it for a whole twenty minutes? It became clear that to love another, required every part of me to be fully present, only then could I be a channel for unconditional love.

Another question came to mind. How often and for how long had I loved myself? I recalled the wise words that Solomon had given me regarding love: *"Self-love must be acquired so that the force can flow through you. Whenever you are being present you are connected to the force, then love is also present. Whenever you love, you are enlightened and a universal channel for love!"*

Some three and a half months had now passed since the onset of my spiritual crash and big steps forwards had been taken in my spiritual development. I felt that it was important to continue to master my logical faculties to help stabilise the left hemisphere for greater right brain orientation. From such a foundation I knew I could receive higher consciousness activity without becoming lost or disorientated. I began to observe my friends and family in a new light by observing if our behaviour patterns were similar in any way. This broadened my outlook, and I began to study and analyse the society I lived in.

It became more noticeable how people interacted with each other or not. There was a general kindness, but much judgment was also present. I could tell if a person was being ego driven or if jealousy was present where envy played a role. Self-study helped me to understand if I was holding any of these negative energies. Through self-analysis I discovered that I had several negative aspects. The mirror showed that judgment and jealousy were major issues that I had to transform. I realised that I needed to clear the logic of its darkness otherwise the ego would continue to overshadow my divinity.

The realisation that judgment is a logical perception that creates separation opened a door for me. My logical eye perceives life as being either black or white just as judgment emanates from the belief in right or wrong! In this manner my logic created preferences which either referred to experience of past happenings or futuristic fear; both were a form of conditioning. The realisation that I had judged a person to be negative because a friend of mine told me he was, was for me, no longer acceptable behaviour. Yes, my friends' negativity had influenced my logic to believe that their judgment of another was true and I made it mine; their thoughts had literally become mine. Their thoughts had possessed me, made me negative towards a person I had not yet met. Why was I giving my power away in the belief that my friends' judgment of another was true?

With this insight, I began to see people from within my own perception and to not prejudge them or judge them purely from external appearances. This approach quickly transformed my attitude towards judging what was right or wrong, into first accepting, and this allowed me to be present. The knowledge that nothing is ever black or white, was enough to empower my own perceptions of life in general. I realised that my prejudgment of others had in reality, prevented me from experiencing and exploring many things with other people.

I became happy for people's good fortune at work or life in general. Previously I had been jealous of a former girlfriend. The way I behaved and responded during our relationship came flooding back to me as a wave of negativity. I began to study my own jealousy, which opened the door to greater self-realisation of how destructive an energy jealousy is. I now saw that my jealousy was based on certain insecurities, which were chiefly emotionally based. There was a fear of not being perfect, not being good enough. Good enough for who or what?

One day I caught myself being jealous of a friend who seemed to have everything materialistically. The emotions quickly rose to activate an old fear of not being worthy of wealth. I also felt that this form of jealousy was older than the few years I had been living on earth. It felt like there was a pattern of past life experiences that required transforming and healing. On that same day, the mirror reflected on to me and I experienced another person being jealous of me. He believed that I was a lover of his divorced wife. It was so intense with him that he became an emotional thinker and the reasoning of logic, the right or wrong, went out through the window. Fear and anger replaced his rational thoughts. He had become logically unstable.

Whatever I said to him, it made it worse, the anger increased, his whole body was shaking, and his face had become red like a ripe apple as he continued to demonstrate his irrational thoughts. His life like mine once was, had been consumed by the jealous fear of losing what he had been controlling, his former wife. False accusations flooded out of his mouth as the energy of jealousy consumed his whole being. He was no longer a loving caring person but had become a demon.

As the anger vented itself the storm passed, and in

a matter of minutes it was gone, but the aftermath remained. The unspoken distrust had been building up and had to find its release; me being the target of his fears. The bars of jealousy were his prison, which prevented the natural flow of spirit and soul energies to blend and love equally. I felt his guilt and shame build as he stood there half realising what he had done. There was a faint smell of alcohol and his eyes were rolling as he struggled to stand still. Then I got a whiff of hashish or marihuana. I tried to think what to do next. Across the narrow street some people had stopped to observe the drama in this usually quiet part of Aberystwyth.

The next day I realised that this could no longer continue, and I went into a meditation to get spiritual guidance. I connected to my main guide who guided me to a temple where a door opened that gave me a view of when I first felt rejected. At last, I could clearly understand the root cause of my jealousy.

From the insight obtained, I was able to forgive the one who had rejected me and began the process of forgiving myself for controlling others through my own jealousy. I spent the next six months looking at and transforming the emotional body in response to my jealous side. Gradually I developed a clear mental attitude to lift my insecurities from the emotional body into the heart, which helped to transform my jealousy. I also decided not to play any more emotional games with others, myself included. Gradually I began to feel different from within; it was as if a veil had been lifted as I applied new values into my life. Joy and happiness filled my life instead of expectations and disappointment.

Seven months later I went to a local town to buy some new clothes. As I walked down the main street, I saw an ex-girlfriend walking towards me, arm in arm with her new boyfriend. I could see that they were happy together. This filled my heart with joy; not so long-ago jealousy would have been there. I had received confirmation of my own transformation; the shadow of jealousy had been lifted. This was a new realisation. My former girlfriend and I looked at each other and smiled as we passed. I sent them a thought of wishing them well. I turned for a moment just after they had passed and saw that their embrace became stronger, and I knew that they had received my positive thought.

The next morning, I awoke feeling extremely clear in mind and body. I reflected on some words I had read a few months back: *"There are two things that money cannot buy, peace of mind and joy of heart. If you have these qualities, then you are rich indeed."* I was beginning to understand the importance of being logically stable, and how it can be obtained and held whilst being in a higher dimension of thought.

Through my observations of others, I saw how some members of my immediate family lived their lives from a strong logical perspective, but with good intentions coming from their heart. There was a certain pride in what they had done in their lives. They often gave generously without seeking reward. They spoke their truth as they saw it to be and as such were open in their honesty. At times, some judgment would come through, but it was not malicious, more factual. I recognised those moments of when they were present in judgment and I wondered if this was logical truth expressing itself as they saw it to be? Yes, was the answer that came flooding back to me. Logical stability has these qualities too.

It was a comfort to me to recognise that people from all walks of life can live their lives being logical and reflecting their spirituality. The simple act of sharing what little one may have is an expression of spirituality.

People from all walks of life are being spiritual without knowing. Maybe it's because the logic does not see thoughts and actions as being spiritually orientated?

Two of my uncles had often asked me if there really was such a place as Heaven? Did we continue to live after death? Would we meet our relatives on the other side? My reply was always a faithful yes!

My uncles and I had many interesting discussions related to spiritual matters, simply because they were curious, but more deeply I felt that they already knew the truth from what they had already experienced before, and had forgotten. I had some insight of this matter into how death plays an important role in removing past life memories, which could otherwise interfere with the opportunities that this current life presents.

Through my inner spiritual dialogue, it became much clearer why I was experiencing events such as meditation with others. There are people in all walks of life that have the same curiosity, and just like me, they too were waking up to the greater possibility of their own levels of spiritual development. Through my personal experiences I felt that I was on the right path to establishing a balanced mind, left and right hemispheres; something of key importance for my spiritual development.

I continued to focus on being grounded, so that I could interact harmoniously with the higher mental activity which was progressively becoming stronger. I felt that the mind was becoming aligned through methods of meditation and contemplation, which were giving me true spiritual insight. Greater access to universal wisdom began to flow harmoniously through my consciousness. There would no longer be any overloading, fast tracking or taking too much on. None of these previous errors occurred. Logical stability during my spiritual development was now establishing itself as I continued to develop a greater faith and understanding.

The energy that came to me, felt like a wave coming to shore or the apple falling to the ground. I had landed. I was ready to continue with my spiritual development, so I set myself eleven guidelines to abide by:

- Always be true to yourself.
- Always stay present.
- Never fear anything or anyone.
- Love others as you would love yourself.
- Take right actions.
- Never judge another.
- Never expect anything.
- Respect others for their differences.
- View the idea of suffering through spiritual values.
- See the beauty in all aspects of life, even in death.
- Remain peaceful, loving, positive and joyous in whatever I do.

# Chapter 6

## Spiritual Guidance

I had moved into a wing of a mansion that a friend of mine owned. It was vacant and at present they needed a housekeeper The timing was perfect because I had put the thought out to find a place a few weeks earlier. I needed to be alone, a place of reclusion which would help my recuperation and development. The mansion was of the 13th Century, and was set in a wooded area that overlooked a ravine, through which the river Teifi ran. Just across the ravine lived my friend Mark, but to get to his place took some ten minutes along some twisty country roads by motorbike.

My living quarters were exceptionally large. The bedroom had three bay windows that were some twelve feet high. The bedroom was south-west facing and over-looked the valley. The kitchen was equally large with slate floors, a very, large kitchen table and benches, and an Aga that ran on oil. I felt blessed to have been offered such a place to stay in. I tried to work out if Karma was being played out here but found no answer, so I just accepted that this must be right for me now.

It was late summer, the end of September, just before the green leaves develop their fuller autumn brown, letting gravity do its work to replenish the earth. That night in bed, I was bathed in moonlight and felt caressed by it's light. It was a perfect sleeping place.

I awoke to the melody of bird song. The sunlight

warmed my left foot at the bottom of my king-sized bed, which I had relocated by pushing it into the bay of the windows. I quickly got washed and dressed and made my way to the kitchen. The water took only a few minutes to boil in the kettle. I sat down to a cup of strong tea and toast for breakfast. I had decided to pay a visit to one of my favourite hills that overlooked the village of Newport. I had been there many times with Mark. I had felt that it was a special place but had not ventured deeper into its mysticism. Today was the day to do that. Down went the tea and toast and I was heading for the coast road that led to the hills on my trusted Triumph motorbike. It was a beautiful late summer's day; the sun was warm and light quality superbly sharp as a razors edge.

Some twenty minutes later I arrived at my destination. I pushed down on the parking leg of the bike and she leaned over to rest, we had arrived. I looked up towards the summit of Blue Stone hill, which rose some 1,300 feet. Not a big hill, but as with many things in life, I had learnt that size is often irrelevant. It's the energy that's important.

On this late Tuesday morning there were very few sheep to be seen cropping the already short grass, and even fewer people, none in fact. I felt that today seemed to be different and stood for a moment to reflect upon my feelings regarding this journey of discovery. I felt the strong pull of the hill and continued to make my way up to the summit. I stopped halfway up for a moment's pause. Some ten yards to my left stood a small yew tree rooted in a slew of rocks. I was in awe of how nature clings onto life. Where there seemed to be no life, life was being created. I looked up the steep, rock strewn slope. How did all these rocks of various sizes get here? To me, there didn't seem to be a logical reason as to how they were here. There were no obvious quarries around, just a mound of blue rocks.

I continued and reached the summit of Blue Stone, and pausing to fill my very being with the energy of the land that surrounded me, the sky and ocean too. Yes, the ocean, the Irish Sea was also visible on this glorious day. I could literally see for miles in any given direction. There were other visible summits that stood out like beacons. It seemed a bit like 'Lord of the Rings' where the beacons were lit as a form of message. My intention came flooding back, there was only one place I wanted to be right now and that was among the stars. I was on a mission. I looked around the mounds of rock that were scattered about me to find the perfect one to sit on for the purpose of meditation. Whilst I searched the same thought kept popping up in my mind. How did these blue rocks get here? From my research into local history, I knew that they had a strong connection to Stonehenge as well as the many local burial chambers of megalithic Wales. They must be special in some form or other, but how and why?

My eye fell itself upon what I felt to be the right meditation stone and I consciously made my way over to pick it up. It was perfect, large enough but not too big. It was also concaved; great to sit on. I then made my way around the small summit to see if anyone else had decided to be here. No one was in sight; perfect for an uninterrupted meditation. I felt the magnetic field of the hill was strong today and I searched for a suitable spot to have my creative visualisation meditation. I closed my eyes and focused my thoughts on seeking a strong energy point for meditating. In my mind's eye I saw that there was a strong light coming from my right, that was powerful, but steady in it's energy. I knew it was a magnetic vortex that was projecting its energy upwards into the universe at that precise time. I made my way to this spot and laid my meditation stone down to sit facing the ocean. I closed my eyes and within seconds I felt my psyche being uplifted. A tingling sensation ran down my entire spinal cord and up to the crown of my head. Wow this was strong! I telepathically asked the universe for guidance and insight regarding this particular location on Blue Stone. I asked about its significance. How had all these rocks been placed here?

A moment later my main guide appeared. He began to explain in his characteristic deep rich voice: *"The blue stones of this hill and the one next to it, to your right, had significant importance 3,500 years ago. They are connected to Stonehenge. The original size of Stonehenge in those times was much, much bigger. At that time, a group of Higher Beings known as Vitrumai, came to earth to teach the wise[10] among the humans how to raise their consciousness. The blue stone of this hill and the one behind you hold a specific vibration that is strongly connected to a particular galaxy within this universe. It's where the Vitrumai, the higher beings, have their world, a world much like this one, you call earth."*

I tried to feel and visualise more deeply what I was being told and shown by my main guide. "What was the purpose of Stonehenge? There is much speculation and logical reasoning as to how the blue stone were transported to Stonehenge."

*"These are very deep questions you are asking, but I can see that you are now ready to receive such insight because you are able to hold the higher frequency of light that comes with its responsibility. I will continue. But stay focused, as you are doing*

---

10 The wise were the Shamans and Druids who had practiced and evolved spiritually for thousands of years.

*so well. The higher beings of Vitrumai are master builders, builders that go far beyond the limited technology of earth people, even of today where mechanical implements are used. Levitation was used as a means to transport the stones from here to Stonehenge. It's one of the simplest ways to move any object when you learn how to master mind over matter, it's simply a matter of vibration transformation. Stonehenge was and still is, to a lesser degree, a deeply significant sacred area. As crude as it is in its appearance, today it still holds much magic and has a meaning for all humans on earth, today as it did then. It had two chief purposes. Firstly it was used as a portal for the higher beings to travel back and forth from earth to their world, which is known throughout this universe as Hernoma. Many of the wise ones in the British Isles experienced such a journey to Hernoma and back, as did your Merlin of Wales. The second function was to allow other higher dimensional beings to visit and explore the earth's atmospheric resonance to export certain materials to create other worlds in other dimensions."*

Wow, I thought, that's far out there in scientific terms.

*"You're quite correct in your thinking but let me give you another insight. The very mound you are sitting on was a dumping ground for the stones and rocks which were of no use for Stonehenge and other locations. These very stones you are sitting on were also lifted from the rock face that still stands a half mile behind you to the south."*

*"What do you mean 'lifted'?"*

*"Here's the bigger picture."*

The next thing I saw was a very, large saucer shaped space craft coming towards me. It was silent, other than a small whistling sound. Its blue-grey belly opened and out poured tons of blue stone, but it was simply a holographic image of what had occurred thousands of years ago.

"Ok, I now understand that history has got it all wrong. Right?"

*"Partly so. The fact is that Stonehenge is still there, just as you are here now. Many of the key stones are still in place, which is why it feels so powerful to those who are tuned more deeply into the energy lines that connect to it, as well as the vortexes that are eternally linked to universal consciousness. This should help confirm to you that there still is definite progress being made towards raising the consciousness of humans. The curiosity it creates helps to stimulate people towards their own inner journey. The mystic can never be deciphered by logical application; the vibration that is there resonates on a much higher vibration."*

"But why are we, I mean humans, so caught up theorising about these very stones, and others nearby such as at Avebury. The logic explanation is that the stones from Stonehenge were moved by means of leavers, rollers, and sheer man-animal power. Isn't that true?"

*"I have already explained and to a degree shown you how higher forces work, and those that understand how to move and use various forms of energy have used it for the greater good. These higher beings have not come to destroy or control but to help create and raise the consciousness of earth beings*

*away from the hold that the evil and negative forces such as the ego have in place. The illusion of the ego that created the Devil or evil as it is known, was created to keep people in fear and in the shadow, out of the light. To live life without the illusion of ego, brings earth beings back into the light!"*

"Oh, I get the bigger picture. Is that why many of the standing stones at Avebury were broken and destroyed by fire, splitting them into smaller pieces? This has been the human approach. Was this because they were ignorant to the facts of how to use a sacred place, which compounded their fear, or was it the evil, the dark side at work here? What about the Pyramids then, who built those?" I was really on fire now and wanted to know everything.

*"Wait a moment; take a deep breath to help ground yourself ... Good now you look better, your energy field – aura – is so strong now. Let's not get carried away. For now, I can only tell you that ignorance is a lack of knowledge, and knowledge without love and light is empty, and has no substance. Yes, to a great degree the knowledge had been lost over the centuries, but it was there, the people of earth have forgotten how to access it. This is how the dark side works to manipulate human consciousness through fear, which is purely a logical perception. The pyramids were built by beings other than the ones who established Stonehenge, the Vitrumai beings."*

I felt that my main spiritual guide was pulling back from the vibration of the meditation I was holding. I accepted that it was time to end the meditation and gradually returned to normal 3D consciousness. I reconnected to the earth through my physical senses and slowly opened my eyes to be blessed once again with the kiss of sunlight. I did not know how long I had sat there reflecting upon my meditation. I was so happy that I had re-established a strong link with my main guide and was blown away by the deep insight given into how universal laws operate on earth. I had a feeling of being reborn, seeing the world through new eyes, a truly holistic universal view.

When I woke up the next day, I was excited to tell Mark about my meditation experience A few hours later I was knocking on his door. The door opened and we embraced each other as usual and a pot of tea was soon on the table.

"You're looking good", said Mark.

"Yes, I feel great, and I want to tell you why." I told him about the meditation and the guidance I had received the day before. Mark listened in silence, but his facial expression spoke volumes. He nodded at times, in agreement, as I explained my journey and experiences during the trip to the hill. I ended my story by feeling relieved, having shared it with someone who understood the language. Sharing it also brought up new insights of the whole experience through my spiritual eye.

I sat back into my chair and waited for Marks response. He paused for a few minutes to gather his thoughts, took another sip of tea, and said: "I feel what you have told me is right because at times I too have meditated there, and during those moments I was also given deep esoteric insight, which is why I can confirm what you have said to be true."

I felt all warm and comforted by his words. and asked him: "What do you know about the pyramids in Egypt?"

Mark went into a contemplative mode, then replied:

"Just like you I have always had a fascination with the pyramids. Do you know that even with today's technology they would be unable to build the pyramids to the accuracy that they were built then? It's just impossible for a number of reasons, time being one. They could not have been built in the twenty years that archaeologists claim, there is not a machine on earth that can cut those slabs of stone as accurately as they are, let alone move them and position them so precisely. The stones of the great Pyramid of Khufu, at Giza in Egypt weigh between 2.3 and 70 tons each. It is estimated that it took 2.3 million such stones to build the Cheops pyramid in Giza. It is claimed that this pyramid was built in 2560 BC and was completed before the Prince of Peace[11] entered Egypt. It's still a great mystery, just as Stonehenge is. Maybe that's a good thing, because what would such technology be used for today? More wars I suppose. The consciousness of today is quite different now because I believe that there is a stronger presence of ego, fear and the dark being held by many. These are the forces that would misuse the knowledge to obtain greater control. Humans would be totally lost and under the control of the dark side and evil, if such knowledge were present today. The atom bomb would seem like a firework compared to the technology that the higher beings have and, I believe, are capable of using."

I pondered his words for a few moments to find the right question.

"So what are your own thoughts about the pyramids? Were they built by human beings as is claimed by geologists, or were there other forces at play here? I understand that the most accepted construction hypotheses by geologists and others are based on the idea that the pyramids were built by manual labour, moving the huge stones from a quarry by dragging them along

---

11 The Prince of Peace came from the Aegean Islands in Greece.

rollers and using leavers and pulleys to lift them into their correct place.”

Again, Mark went into deep thought for some moments before raising his head and saying: “Let’s ask upstairs shall we?”

I merely nodded in agreement, and we both settled down in preparation for a meditation.

“It’s good to have you back on the right path again Ralph.”

I smiled back at Mark and nodded in agreement. We were now beyond words.

I got into my comfortable sitting position with my back straight. I understood that this position gave a clearer channel for the kundalini to flow along the spinal cord and through the chakras. I closed my eyes and took a few deep breaths, consciously filling myself with light to help clear anything negative that I may be holding. Then I opened my consciousness to receive a greater flow of universal energy, light. In a flash I had decided to return to a special place where I could meet my main spiritual guide, and sure enough my guide was there. We greeted each other in the usual manner with thoughts of love. The telepathic dialogue began by my guide saying to me: *“I have been listening to your conversation with Mark. It’s great to see that you are back on track.”*

“It doesn’t seem as if I have been away?”

*“In one aspect you haven’t. The timescale on earth is vastly different to that of the universal clock. The earth timeline is on a different time scale.”*

“Well, I’m happy to be here with you at this moment. Now please tell me all there is to know about the Egyptian pyramids. I want to know, I want to see, how it was when they were being built and used."

A flash of light appeared in my mind's eye, and I found myself facing the main pyramid of Khufu's in Giza with the Sphinx behind me in its full glory. It was carved out of a single piece of stone weighing hundreds of tons and is over 200 feet in length.

There was much activity taking place with hundreds, if not thousands, of Egyptians working to build the new foundation of another pyramid that stood some 300 feet next to the completed pyramid of Khufu's. I noticed that there were three different types of beings walking around. From what I could tell, there were human beings of average height, and then there was another type that was at least two meters tall with slightly differing body structure, much slimmer, longer arms and legs. The third race of beings were at least three meters tall; they were enormous. They too had slim arms and legs with a slightly elongated torso, long necks and heads that were more oval. There were very few of this type, who seemed to be in charge of the others. Their headdresses were like the ones depicted in the hieroglyphics that are found there today. The taller beings had a different aura about them. They seemed to be unaware of my presence and I understood that no one could see me in the vibration I was holding. I also realised that I needed further guidance, so I called upon my main guide.

"Can you explain to me what is going on here? Who are these beings? Where do they come from and why are they here?"

*"Wait please, one question at a time. You have come back in time, it is now the year 4720 B.C. and the*

*pyramid you see, is called Khufu, which by the way means ship. This pyramid has just been completed. The foundations to the one on your left have not long been started; they are still in the process of excavating the inner chamber that goes one hundred feet into the core of the vortex. There is still much to do."*

"Now it is you who are giving me too much information. We have come back in time? Are we in a hologram?"

*"Yes, we are. Every moment and event are recorded in the matrix of universal consciousness, which can be extracted to guide and help for the greater good."*

"And the vortex that you mentioned, how is that connected to the pyramid and burial chamber?"

*"As you know, the energies of the many vortexes on earth are significant because they help maintain the electromagnetic field, as well as being a direct line to universal consciousness and can be used as such."*

I could feel my energies becoming stronger through receiving such knowledge. "Well, who are these taller beings, they seem to be different from the humans, not only in stature but also in appearance. Why? Where do they come from?"

*"These higher beings are known throughout the universes as the 'Salasiani people. They come from the fifth universe and 88$^{th}$ Galaxy. Their world needs certain minerals that are still quite abundant here on earth. They have deemed it worthwhile to return and excavate what they can, without destroying the natural balance of the earth's eco system."*

"They have been here before?"

*"Oh yes, the Sphinx was created by them some nine thousand years previously, along with other artefacts that are no longer visible directly on the surface of earth."*

"Were they good or bad? Oh, excuse me, this is not a logical concept. They seem to be friendly. Were they? Are they?"

*"Yes, they were and still are. The Salasiani were deemed to be Gods by the local inhabitants because they literally came out of the sky. They descended with their technology and put it to good use, as you can see now."*

"The locals must have been terrified when they first landed."

*"They were but that was soon put right. The Salasiani produced food and water out of nowhere. That helped the local inhabitants to survive through a deep famine that had been taking place for a decade. Climate change was just entering a new phase, which was the result of the nuclear wars involving negative aliens, some fifty-six thousand years previously. The local inhabitants had been struggling to survive for many decades before the arrival of the Salasiani race."*

"The pyramid is enormous. How long has it taken to build, and why so big?"

*"With the Salasiani technology, this pyramid was built in less than four earth years. This may be hard*

*to believe but look over there at how that fifty ton rock is being moved with ease!"*

I stood in awe as this precision cut slab of rock was being levitated and positioned at the corner of the new pyramid.

My guide continued: *"It's important to bear in mind that the size of this pyramid here on earth is small compared to the ones they have on their home planet called Swz. That translates to 'Sky' by the way."*

"Tell me, how big are the pyramids on Swz?"

*"To put it into correct perspective, you can see the size of Khufu; it is approximately twenty times smaller than the ones they have on Swz."*

"What are they used for? Why do they build them?"

*"The Salasiani people have no direct need for a home or house, as is the tradition here on earth. They live collectively sharing what they have equally, just as the tribal native people have and some still do on earth. Can you imagine that the entrance of one of their main pyramids on Swz is 520 yards wide and 70 yards tall? Can you see it?"*

"Oh yes, it's enormous. There are much smaller pyramids on either side of the entrance, what are they used for?"

*"Those are approximately the size of Khufu, which gives you a true perspective of how big this main pyramid of Swz is! The smaller pyramids to either side help hold the vibration of the main pyramid;*

*there are two others on the opposite ends, which you can't see from here. These lesser pyramids are also used for what you term self-development or raising consciousness. Everything can be found within the main pyramid on Swz. It's a place of study, rest, play, sleep, eat and play again. There is a Master being connected to each main pyramid, who is known as Serima. Each Serima is an infinitely wise being who is directly in touch with other beings on other dimensions. The Salasiani beings are known for their passive approach but are strong and will use their knowledge and power accordingly."*

"So why are they here?"

*"They are here to predominantly collect Gold and Lithium. The gold plays an important part in their reflector shield that eliminates ultraviolet light frequencies not commonly found in this galaxy and universe. This is why gold is so valued by them; it is not used as a symbol of wealth as it is on Earth. The Lithium is also a lifesaver for them. It's an important element in preventing cellular deterioration. The Salasiani can live for several hundred years on Swz, which is drastically reduced when on Earth due to Earth's bacterial and biological content."*

"I can see that they are using lasers to cut the rocks, whilst others are levitating them to their exact positions. Is there anything that they are not capable of?"

*"You are of course right in your observation, but they do have a limited time in this environment. Every seven days they return to their mother ship, which is about 26,000 miles out in space. They must return to detoxify themselves for one earth day, which*

*is relatively a short period before returning to continue their work. The atmosphere on earth is heavy in bacteria and other pollutants. It is quite different from Swz, which is purer. They were better prepared for this return trip after their first visit, just over 6,000 years ago. But they do like being here. They told me, each one has volunteered for this trip of a lifetime."*

"You can communicate with them? Why haven't you told me?"

*"Tune in and you too will communicate."*

In the next moment I was listening to their dialogue but was unable to decode it. One of the leaders picked up on my frequency and asked my guide to clarify my position, which was duly done.

"This is 4720 B.C. right?"

*"Yes"*, replied a Salasiani leader.

"How much longer will you, the Salasiani, stay on earth?"

*"For another 300 years."*

"You seem so sure of your answers?"

*"That is true, but it's not as clear cut as it seems. Some of our leaders have interbred to become more humanised; it's a way of integrating the genetics. You see, those lesser Salasiani beings, they were the first to be interbred through human genetics. They are much smaller in size now and have a more refined body that resembles the perfectionism of the human's*

*physical body. Real progress is being made on all levels throughout the many worlds. You earth beings are not alone, never have been. The relics of us are still very noticeable in the hieroglyphics we left! There is much wisdom that has not yet been evaluated due to the lack of intelligence. It will not be found by logical analysis alone."*

"I have always felt that only a small piece of the truth had been revealed by geologists and alike. Will Salasiani beings ever return?"

*"This is our last trip to earth; partly because we have engineered what is required to restore and replenish our Lithium and shield that protect our planet. We also believe that the earth beings will eventually resolve their differences."*

"Well that's good to hear but I have another question. Why are there so many human beings here? They don't seem to have been enslaved as many historical books state."

*"You know, even in this primitive world, word travels fast. Some came out of curiosity, others as a means to survive; many are here because of the good food and lifestyle. They are cared for by us Salasiani beings. For this they do some work, such as filling in the small crevasses left after a block of stone was positioned. They also help cultivate food for the thousand or more workers. There were not so many workers as your history books state, because nothing too heavy was manually lifted. De-gravitation methods took care of the heavy work. The large rocks were of course impossible to cut with chisels as is claimed. Do you really believe that these rocks were*

*precision cut without special metal implements?"*

"I am beginning to believe it!"

*"It's true that most of the artwork and Hieroglyphics were done by hand, the rest not. Lasers were used."*

"Wow, okay. There is much speculation about how the Pharaohs used certain rituals. Can you please enlighten me on this subject?"

*"It's a good question. Mummification is native to us on Swz. One of our Salasiani leaders died whilst on earth and was duly mummified and placed in a tomb within a pyramid. This was to ensure that his soul may journey back home to reincarnate. The Pharaohs of the day were deeply touched by this tradition and wanted to emanate how the Swz leaders were respected, even after death, which is why so many Pharaohs were mummified in Egypt."*

"Now that's history in the making, isn't it?"

*"It is."*

"Can you clear up another mystery and explain to me how you manage to see inside the Pyramids? After all there are many beautiful works of art there. There seems to be no evidence of fires or torches being used because there are no traces of ash or smoke in the ceilings."

*"Well, let's keep it simple. The geometrical form of the Pyramid helps create an energy field that blends the ionised energy with the electrical vortex that runs up the core of the pyramid. This energy, which*

*we call vixs, then illuminates the specially adapted lanterns by transforming the etheric particles within the vacuum lamps. It's a never-ending natural form of energy which remains active for as long as the pyramids stay intact. Every passageway, every chamber, was illuminated in this way. When we returned, we also took the lamps with us because they would have been a danger if they were not maintained properly."*

"Wow, that's amazing. But why aren't we able to create this today or use this technology?"

*"The human being may get there one day, but there is much that the scientists of today are missing, many are looking in the wrong direction. However, there is a light there; three independent scientists have come together somewhere in Mexico and are now producing petrol form thin air, which is most definitely a step in the right direction."*

I could feel that my meditation time was drawing to an end. I gave my thanks for the guidance I had received from the Salasiani elder and my main guide and I gradually returned myself to where I was seated. I opened my eyes again, to see that Mark was silently watching me.

"Where have you been?" he said. "I have been watching you for over half an hour now, it felt like it was a deep journey you were on!"

"It was! What a journey - amazing insights - I'm blessed and thankful."

Mark then said: "Let's have a cup of tea first before sharing."

He headed for the kitchen. I remained seated unable

to move. I took a drink of water from the glass that had been placed next to me by Mark prior to the meditation. The sip of water felt good and helped to ground my energies. I moved my legs and stood up after a few minutes and went to see how Mark was doing in the kitchen. Tea was made and we stepped out into the back yard to share our experiences during the meditation, as we often did.

"I don't know about you Ralph, but that was an amazingly deep one for me. My main guide came and showed me a number of past lives, ones in which we, you and I, shared in positive ways. They were all Native American Indian past life experiences. We are truly spirit Brothers."

I could see that he was deeply touched by his meditation experience and we hugged each other with deep respect.

"Well Mark, the bonding still continues. We have only good Karma now, let's keep shining!"

"I'm all for that!"

We continued to share for an hour or more before I headed home. I went straight to bed and slept like a baby.

# Chapter 7

## Guidance of Another Kind

A couple of years had now passed since I had left the Mansion. I had planned to spend the summer travelling from one musical festival to another throughout the U.K. It was early July and my third festival. I was in Sussex heading towards the 1989 'Big Green' gathering; a music festival. I had just arrived at the location of the festival after a couple of days hitch-hiking from Wales with good weather. Following the map on my ticket, I made my way along an open track across open fields that led to the festival entrance. There was noticeably a strong presence of police on the outer and inner entrance of the main gate. I duly handed my ticket to the gate attendant and passed onto the ridge of a very large open field, which I estimated to be approximately fifty acres.

The police were busy body-searching the festival goers for drugs; chiefly marihuana and hashish. After passing through, I stood a hundred or so yards away from the entrance to observe and feel the energy of the land and the people coming into the field. I noticed that there was also a police bus being used to strip search those who were deemed by the police to be highly likely in in possession of drugs. Many people were gathering around the bus and started loudly shouting for its removal. A couple of new suspects were hawled into the bus and the door was quickly closed. Then some men and women climbed onto the roof of the bus and started to jump up and down.

More and more people gathered around the bus and were beginning to rock it whilst those on top began to strip off their clothes. In a minute or two some seven people were stark naked on top of the bus and were leaping up and down to demonstrate their disapproval. This continued for some minutes, then the side door of the police bus opened and out came the suspects half naked cheering and jeering. They were treated like martyrs by the crowd. Then the engine of the police bus was fired, and a plum of black smoke bellowed out from the exhaust. It started to move forward and those on the roof quickly jumped off. It was heading towards the gate entrance. Some police quickly opened the gate and the bus disappeared down the track followed by the remaining police officers in their cars. There was euphoria, a sense of liberty. It was a powerful moment for me too. Live and let live.

I found a suitable spot to pitch my tent that I had been allocated according to my ticket. There were hundreds of tents already set up in this predominantly chalky field. My two-man tent was up in a matter of minutes and I felt that I had chosen a comfortable space; the entrance faced the east to greet the rising sun. This was the first day of five and I was keen to explore what seemed to me to be a very, large festival. The organis-ers said that they were expecting up to five thousand gatherers for this particular event. I had been to two previous festivals with approximately 500 attendants; this was my first attendance at such a large festival. But it felt good to be here, and I embraced the air and atmosphere with joy.

It was late afternoon and I decided it was time for a walkabout. There were many large tents; some resem-bled circus tents that used to come to my town when I was a boy. From what I could tell some were being used for bands of various kinds, but there was a main tent that held the centre stage and I headed in that general direction. As I passed the main tent, I came to a small incline that ran alongside the main field. There was an archway of branches and flowers that had a poster that read 'Healing Field'. I entered and walked along the pathway through the numerous tents that ran along either side. It was well organised with good spaces between the tents. Each tent or marquee was clearly sign posted, there were a number of cafes there too. There was a good choice of therapists from massage, to shiatsu, hands-on healing, and Tarot readings. There was even a tent offering psychotherapy. I really felt at home amongst these good people.

I was feeling hungry and during my walkabout, I had already decided which cafe was right for me. The marquee that I had chosen was Bedouin based. It was quite beautiful to look at with long flowing canvases of differing colours. There were large open spaces with piles of cushions of different kinds scattered about. I checked out the menu; all food was vegetarian, great. I chose my dish and looked for a suitable place in the semi-full cafe. I found a little corner and plonked my ass.

There were lively conversations taking place all around me, which filled the space with a pleasant vibration. No one was speaking in a loud fashion. It was interesting to feel the energy of this space and the souls in it. A guy sat opposite me and was talking to a couple of his friends. He suddenly noticed me and introduced himself as Mike. We duly shook hands, and I was briefly introduced to his friends Peter, Kim and Katrin. We quickly got into a conversation about the festival program.

"The big red tent in the middle of the festival is where most of the action is taking place", explained Mike.

"What kind of action?" I asked.

"Well, there's a bit of a political setup here. The green party is actively trying to stop the latest motorway bypass being built through the countryside not far from here." He quickly continued: "Did you see the police doing a runner this afternoon? Great wasn't it?"

Everybody agreed with a general nod of approvement and a few shudders of amusement.

"How are you fixed Ralph?" asked Katrin.

"Oh, I'm ok thanks. It's my first big festival, and so far, it feels good to be here."

"First big festival, hey. Congrats and welcome", added Peter.

The conversation moved onto a discussion regarding the various bands that were to perform. My newly found friends seemed to be seasoned travellers and festival goers. I mostly listened to their experiences and learnt a lot about being alternative in an increasingly materialistic world. They were good people with good intensions, and it felt like home for now.

Later, I tucked into my sleeping bag and tried to sleep but was disturbed by a steady flow of new arrivals that were setting up their tents. I realised how sound travels easily in the middle of the night, but I did eventually sleep.

The next time I opened my eyes the tent was both light and warm, as the sunlight was penetrating my tent. I lay there for a while just taking in the energy of the morning's atmosphere. I could sense other people around me getting up and going through their body rituals. I skipped breakfast because I did not feel hungry. I now ate when I felt like it; I was no longer governed by the clock to eat at specific times. I unpacked my camping stove and made myself a cup of tea at the entrance of my tent. Sometime in the middle of the night a new tent had been erected right next to mine, and the zipper opened as I took a sip of tea. A guy popped his head out, which was covered with tight blond curly hair. We immediately connected and said hi to each other. I offered him a cup of tea which he quickly accepted, followed by "I'll be out in a moment."

It was a warm morning, and we were both shirtless. He sat next to me and introduced himself as Steven Williamson.

"Is Steve or Steven best for you?" I asked.

"Steve is fine."

We shared some common knowledge of each other's lives. Then Steve reached into his tent and pulled out a Spanish guitar. Great I thought, now I can get my harmonica out too. We sat there for a few hours just jamming and having fun. The zipper of the tent next to Steve's opened and out came a woman who immediately introduced herself as Patsy. Apparently from their body language I could tell that Steve and Patsy were together, but I felt that there was an underlying tension between them. I made some more tea and gave Patsy a cup as we sat discussing life in general. Then the three of us headed off for lunch. Patsy seemed to know several people at the festival and stopped to talk to friends a few times on our short walk to the cafe. It turned out that Steven was a student of economics and Patsy was graduating in environmental studies, hence her link to the Green Party. We had lunch and I decided to go my own way, heading for the main tent.

On my way to the tent, I passed a group of people who were practicing playing the Didgeridoo. This was my first real live experience of listening to the Didgeridoo. It was wonderful to listen to live, and for some minutes I studied how the player's energy integrated with his instrument. I sat down amongst the other watchers and focused on the teacher as he began to play to the expanding group that gathered. I observed his circular breathing and how his in-breath blended with his continuous out breath. As he got deeper into his playing, so did his psyche. In a matter of minutes, he was no longer there in his body, his spirit and soul were flowing through his instrument. I could tell from his energies that he was in a form of trance; he was truly channelling universal consciousness through the sacred breath that created the music. I then began to realise how and why the Aboriginal natives of Australia were so deeply in touch with nature and universal knowledge. Their song lines were paramount to their wellbeing and the environment. They had been playing on those sacred spots for thousands of years. In those moments, I thought of how everything is interconnected through the arts. My experience was reaching from England all the way to Australia. In one sense Australia was here and I closed my eyes and imagined that I was down under. Pictures flooded my mind's eye; I could even smell the outback and feel its energy. Then the music came to an end and everyone applauded the musicians. I intuitively knew that I had been an Aborigine in one or more past lives, but a question came up: "What do I do with this insight?" I knew I would meditate on this, later on.

I had no idea of the time since I had stopped wearing a watch a few years back. I looked up into the sky to see how far the earth had rotated in relation to the sun. It was later than I thought, and another thought entered my mind: This place was like a timeless zone, just like I experienced every time I meditated. Good, another positive sign that I am in the right place. I headed for another cafe that took my fancy. The festival was in full swing now with all kinds of activities taking place simultaneously. There was a juggling act and fire eaters in one area and nearby a few Shamans were giving

Didgeridoo lessons. In another area the Djembe drum was being taught. Something I could try tomorrow.

The food was good and the vegetarian Ratatouille was superb. I approached the big tent, which seemed to be very busy by the volume of sound bellowing out from it. Jazz music seemed to be the favourite, which was being drowned by the sheer noise of people talking. I passed through the tent's entrance and tried to make my way around to one side. There were many people gathered around the entrance. It seemed as if human nature tends to like such meeting spots. I nudged my way through, trying to find a quieter spot. There was a large open bar at the back of the tent, and many were drinking beer and an assortment of alcohol. For me, the energy was a bit heavy, some were drunk, and many were high on drugs. The air was impregnated with Hashish and Marihuana smoke. I heard people mentioning how terrible it was that the bypass was going ahead, and how the activists had been camped out on various parts of the road works trying to stop it. A woman next to me said to her friend: "Some even chained themselves to trees and diggers. Great isn't it?" Her friend nodded in agreement.

A spokesperson stepped onto the stage. There was a big roar, and I wondered who this popular guy could be. I was beginning to feel a bit uncomfortable. The combined energies of the alcohol, various drugs and the psyche within the tent was having a negative effect upon my sensitivity. I thought that I should stay put, see this through, remain calm, and filter all the negative energies. They need not have any effect on my psyche. This accepting line of thought, helped enormously and I began to relax again.

Another man and a woman joined the spokesperson on stage. They began to talk about the major road works that were taking place locally as well as nationally in relation to the harm it was doing to the environment in general. He claimed that the plants and animals were at risk and the general losses of natural habitat were unacceptable. I was in full agreement with their sentiments and the direct action that they were involved in. They continued to talk about the natural habitat as I reflected how this country, the whole of the British Isles had once been covered in forests. This was not a new thing that's taking place, it was almost as old as the nation. I shared these thoughts with a woman. standing next to me, and she nodded in agreement. She introduced herself as Jane.

Gradually over the next hour the energy within this tent began to change from passive to being tinted by aggression. People were indeed angry at the politicians, companies and local councillors who had sanctioned the deforestation and removal of natural habitats. Some of the people began to boo and heckle a spokesperson for seeking a compromise with the authorities. It seemed that many people were becoming more drunk and spaced out with drugs, in a relatively short time. It was becoming ugly. The real debate had lost its edge, where clear thought and decisive steps towards finding solutions had become void of energy. The will to have an open dialogue was lost in a psychic impurity. I turned to Jane and asked: "Would you like to have a cup of tea?"

Smiling, she answered: "Yes, let's go."

A few minutes later we were breathing fresh air. It felt great. It was a clear, starry night. Jane and I walked along the main fairway of the festival, which was still rather busy. Campfires were burning in front of the major stalls with groups of people sharing their life experiences. A young man appeared from the shadowy night light and approached us holding what looked like a round silver platter.

"Want some hash-balls? They're only a quid!"

"No thanks", I replied.

With my rejection, he faded back into the night, which was surreal. We found a cafe and viewed the choice of teas. I opted for a black Chai and Jane went for the green Ceylon tea. After a short time, I got up to collect and pay for the teas and returned to continue the conversation. I asked Jane: "What are hash-balls?'"

She gave me a broad smile with a sparkle in her eyes.

"This really is your first time here", she said. "Hash-balls are a form of pure Hashish that is mixed with alcohol and boiled with a little water until the water and alcohol evaporate. It is then allowed to cool, which leaves a sticky residue, this is then rolled into small balls and placed in a fridge or freezer."

"Wow, that's pretty heavy isn't it?"

"Oh yes, but it depends on the quality of the Hashish of course."

"Have you tried one?"

"Yes, but not for a long time, I want to take care of my body, my temple, so to speak."

"I'm happy to hear that", I replied.

We began to discuss what we felt had taken place in the big tent just now. I continued: "I know many of the people in there have good hearts and their intensions are right, but something is missing, something doesn't feel right to me."

"You're right, I feel the same way."

There were some moments of silence; we were deep in contemplation when I had a realisation.

"I have it! I now understand why I feel so strongly that something was out of place in that tent. You may think that I'm a purist, but this is what I feel." I began to explain. "They are so focused on saving the environment, even maybe the world, but what about themselves, shouldn't that come first?" I continued without waiting for a response from Jane. "Surly it starts within me, within each of us, my temple must be pure, clear from anything negative. Clear from other chemicals such as alcohol and drugs. Live by example, I say. How is anyone in parliament going to take the issues that are being discussed in the tent seriously when many there, are either intoxicated or are under the influence of narcotics? I have heard many judging the activists as hippies, layabouts, and good for nothing dole scroungers. I am simply observing here. I understand that it's their way of doing things; how they spend their time. How they feel is important for them too. I say save yourself first. Come clean, then the way you decide on will be clearer. You can't see clearly under the fog of drugs like Hashish or Marihuana."

There was a moment's pause as Jane shuffled herself and sat straighter in her chair before responding: "Many of these people are passionate about their cause and beliefs, some are also my friends. I understand exactly where you are coming from Ralph and in one way I agree but in another, not. Yes, to cleanse and remain clear in ones energies is of great importance but we are all on a journey, we are mirrors for each other. You reflect something to me just as I do to you. I believe that everyone knows what their inner calling is on an unconscious level, which can rise to become a conscious matter. I believe this is what spiritual development is, it's the unconscious becoming the conscious, the waking up. These good people are waking up, but more importantly, they are doing it their way."

As I listened, I felt the deep truth of Jane's words penetrating my heart, I was filled with warmth. Jane was much deeper than I had thought. We sat in silence for several minutes as I absorbed what Jane had shared.

"You're spot on there, Jane. It's difficult to change things when the judged judges the judged?"

"Yes, it is", agreed Jane.

Another peaceful moment passed, then I asked:

"What are you doing tomorrow?"

"Not sure, I may have a massage."

"Sounds good, can we meet tomorrow to continue this discussion?"

"Yes, I am sure we will bump into each other somewhere."

I bid Jane good night and headed for my tent. I was tired, and I welcomed the warmth of my sleeping bag; I did not remember falling sleep.

I awoke to the blazing sunlight, that had dramatically raised the temperature in my tent from the night's chill. I quickly opened the zipper, and a waft of fresh air blew into my face. It seemed to be late morning and it was very warm. I had heard the previous night that the general weather forecast had been very good, but this was just great for me, being a sun worshiper. I donned my loose blue linen slacks and headed for the healing area. I sat down on the grass in an open area of a healing field café, to drink my tea. I lifted my head to absorb the sun's rays and sensed that there was much activity around. Many people were topless due to the heat. Some had painted their bodies in contrasting colours, and they looked great. In an open space to my right there were a group of Krishna[12] followers. The previous day they had paraded around the entire camp with their ox and cart, beating the drum and chanting "Krishna, Hare-Krishna". Most of their group were sat around their campfire, fully clothed. From what I understood, nudity is not condoned by any Krishna follower. However adjacent to the Krishna group were a group of some ten nudists who were joyfully painting themselves with body paint. This group was quite loud and active and as such were attracting some attention. They were simply having fun in the activity of

---

12 Hindu God

being free. In the next instant they all started to dance to some music, which continued for several minutes. Then they started to run and were heading straight for the Krishna camp. The brightly painted nudists ran in a line directly through and around the Krishna campfire and around some of the Krishna devotees who were now standing. It was a fantastic moment, everyone in sight of this happening just burst into laughter, me included. It was a unique human moment, but deeply spiritual at the same time. Not one of the Krishna disciples raised an eyebrow. No sense of protest, no objection, one or two even smiled broadly. A sight to remember; complete acceptance of others. I had indeed chosen the right spot for tea that morning.

It was the last day of the festival, and the weather had remained hot. The midday sun baked my bare shoulders as I made my way towards a tent where the Djembes were playing. In a large open space near the centre of the festival there were circus events taking place with a very tall clown on stilts, and some people juggling. Next to the jugglers were a few dogs doing some tricks and others performing spontaneously. It was very colourful and great to watch the various artists.

After some time, I noticed that a large group of fifty or more, were heading through the healing area towards a nearby wood. I was curious and followed instinctively. I joined the group which had grown to around a hundred or more. I asked a man next to me what was going on. He told me that the couple at the front, were going to be married at a pagan ceremony. After walking for about two hundred yards into the wood we arrived at an opening where the sunlight kissed the earth. Everyone positioned themselves to create a circle around the couple. The bride wore a tiara of flowers and had a long flowing dress that was pastel blue. The groom wore an open jacket with striped, blue, red, and yellow trousers. They both looked great. The one holding the ceremony was also casually dressed. No need for dog-collars here. The marriage vows were simple; to respect, love and be true to one another for the next year. I asked a guy next to me who the priest was.

"He's what's known as a rebel priest. He has left the church to follow his heart, to bless people, to serve people without the dogma and politics that control Religion."

A free thinker. Things were changing for the greater good.

Later, I met Jane on my way back to the festival field. She looked great and she also complemented me on my appearance. We shared some more thoughts of the discussion we had had a few nights ago, exchanged addresses and bid each other fairwell.

I had previously arranged to stay with new friends I had made six months previously. I was heading for a village near Alton Barnes in Wiltshire. I wanted to experience Crop Circles at first hand. My rucksack was loaded, and I was ready to go. I made my way to the main road and started to hitchhike. I managed to get a lift on the motorway with travellers and bid them fairwell as they drove off in their converted bus. It was late afternoon, and I was now on a minor road that led off the motorway. I calculated that I was some twenty-five miles away from the house of my friends. I stuck my thumb out to the next car that came along

An hour had passed, and I was still in the same place. It was getting late. I told myself to relax. All is well, enjoy where you are and what you are doing. I did not completely understand the power of thought, but a lorry and two cars later, a car stopped. I ran for the passenger's door, opened it and asked: "Are you going anywhere near Alton Barnes?”

“Yes”, came the immediate reply. “Passing right through it, jump in.”

I quickly opened the back door and laid my heavy rucksack on the back seat, jumped into the front seat and we were off.

“What part of Wales are you from?” asked the driver.

“Oh, from the west coast”, I replied.

“I’m Hanna by the way, what’s your name?”

“Ralph.”

“I went to University at Aberystwyth. Is that near where you live?”

“Yes, I live not far from there”, I replied.

“What brings you to this neck of the woods?”

“I met some people last winter who are researching the Crop Circle phenomena.”

“Well you’re certainly in the right place at the right time. There have been more circles this year than any other year”, responded Hanna.

Great, a new adventure was about to begin. Things were silent for some minutes, then she asked: “What address do you have, where are you staying?”

I opened my address book and read out the name of the house, Oakfield Cottage and the address.

“Ah, I know Jim and Kath. It is Jim and Kath’s place that you are staying, right?” Without my replying she continued: “I’m going right by there. I can drop you off at their doorstep.”

Hanna’s faded red Ford Escort stopped outside the gated entrance of a traditional Wiltshire cottage with its thatched roof, black wooden beams, whitewashed walls, and deep imbedded windows. In the parking area stood a deep blue Volvo estate, that belonged to Jim and Kath, and I knew I was in the right place. I opened my door and went to get my rucksack.

"I can't stop, but please give Jim and Kath my regards. All the best, happy crop circle adventures."

I thanked her, closed the back door, and off she sped.

The name Oakfield Cottage was etched into a board that rested in the hedge next to the double gate entrance. I was somewhere in the countryside, and from what I could see the nearest neighbour was about half a mile away. I rang the back doorbell and was shortly greeted by Kath. She was bubbling: "Great that you are here Ralph... lots of crop circle activity in the last few days... I've booked a helicopter for 8 a.m. tomorrow. I want to take some pictures of the latest circles. I'll use them for the coming calendar. Jim is out getting some groceries. He'll be back shortly. Would you like a cup of tea?"

"That would be great, thanks", I replied.

A moment later the back door opened and in came Jim followed by Nelson, their Scottish Deerhound. We greeted each other and I gave Nelson a pat or two to begin our bonding.

"Great to see you here Ralph, I've, no sorry, *we* have been looking forward to your visit, please treat our home as if it were your own."

I thanked them both for their kind offer and hospitality.

Then Jim said: "I have some new crop circle pictures to show you. Kath has been really busy since the first crop circle appeared in late May, haven't you darling?"

It was wonderful to see how they were sharing their experiences together, such passion for their work. Jim took me into his office where there were a few crop circle photos laid across a large table.

"So far there have been twenty-seven circles; they are becoming more complex each year. Twenty years ago, they were mainly a circle with a single layer, now they are more complex, geometrical designs that have up to five interwoven layers that often go in opposite directions. It helps to highlight the design, especially from above, just as you can see here in these pictures."

We had spent an hour or two discussing the pictures when Kath called us in for supper. In our continuing conversation Kath said: "Tomorrow were going to visit a large crop circle that was reported to us today. Great to have you join us Ralph."

"Nothing would stop me!" I replied.


I awoke to the sound of Nelson barking. It was 9 a.m. and I had overslept. Jim was sitting in the kitchen reading a newspaper.

"Good morning Ralph", said Jim without lifting is head from reading. "Look." He lifted the newspaper in my direction. "They have a very good picture of a crop circle that we visited yesterday, they say it is a hoax, you know, man-made."

"What are your thoughts on that, Jim?"

"Some are rolled out and planked that way yes, but very few. I can easily tell which is man-made and which is not by the stems of the plants. In the man-made ones the plant stems are always broken or damaged due to stamping or using wooden boards to make the pattern. With an original however, that does not happen, the stems are bent or re-formed. From a scientific point of view, there must have been heat present, to bend the stem without force or damage as happens when man-made. No one really knows how or why this phenomenon occurs." Jim went on: "Another fact that helps to disprove and distinguish the original crop circles from a fake one is their complexity and accuracy of design. It would take a day or two for a group of people to even measure the geometrical design correctly, combined with the fact, that walking all over the area would basically flatten much of its core."

The phone rang. Jim answered and I helped myself to some breakfast that had already been prepared by my hosts. Jim seemed to be really excited about something during the phone call. He quickly made some notes and put the phone down.

"Great news Ralph, there is a new circle been reported by one of our members, it's not so far away either. We can go and explore the latest circle soon!"

I felt an electrical charge running through my veins and a tingling sensation ran up my neck. This had to be right.

The phone rang again, Jim picked up, and listened intently, then replied: "Good, see you soon."

Within twenty minutes Kath had arrived. She came rushing in and grabbed a quick cup of tea and some toast, joining our conversation on crop circles.

"It was great up there today; the latest CC is no less spectacular. I estimate it to be between seventy and eighty yards across. It's complex and has several circles outside that follow specific lines that are defined. I can't wait to be in it!"

Within a few minutes we were in the car heading for the location of the latest crop circle. Jim had been given the coordinates and knew the exact place to park the car. He informed me that many farmers were afraid of crop circles; some even cut the crop whenever a new one appeared, even if the crop was not ready to be harvested. He explained, this was partly to stop people walking into their field; but also to avoid media attention on themselves.

Some fifteen minutes later the car stopped behind a green Morris 1000 next to a hedgerow that ran along a single-track road. Jim made sure that there was enough room for other cars to pass. I felt that he did not want to be disturbed when in the circle, which was confirmed when he said: "That looks ok Ralph; others can pass."

There was a gateway just fifteen yards to the front of the cars next to which stood a young man waving. He came up to greet us and we were duly introduced by Jim.

"This is Mathew, Ralph."

We shook hands, both smiling broadly. There was a new feeling building up in my physical body, it was beyond the normal joy one gets on an adventure, it felt so strong in my heart, and head.

As we approached the gate, Mathew said: "I've been here for a couple of hours now and I have not seen anyone else here yet. After I discovered it, I drove down the road to phone you Jim. I came back straight away, so we are the first here."

"That's great", said Kath.

I could tell that everyone was excited by this discovery. It was difficult to see the new crop circle from the road because it was obscured by a little brow some 150 yards away. We followed the tracks laid down by the tractor, in single file, not to damage the green barley that stood strong in this large field. It must have been 50 acres, maybe more. As we approached the circle my psyche was buzzing. I could literally feel the hairs on the back of my neck rise. I stood at the very edge of the circle and closed my eyes to tune more deeply into its energy. The other three were already exploring the circle in their own way. I could hear them walking around. Opening my eyes, I took off my sandals and put them to one side, then stepped into the circle. I could feel the morning dew under my feet. I felt I needed to take in some of the circle's raw energy, so I bent down to take a sip of water that lay on the leaves of the plants. The effect was immediate; it heightened my sensitivity of the circle. With each step I took, it was like walking on frosty ground in winter. There was a crunch, crunch sound that filled every step I took. This was indeed a pristine circle, and we were the first to be in it. I then sat down on a spot that felt strong and closed my eyes to meditate.

Jim and Mathew were already meditating in another area within the circle. In the next second I was flying through the universe, well, an aspect of me was. It was so powerful, that I found myself being connected to a specific planet in a distant galaxy and was given insight into its significance to earth. This explained to me why the crop circle had been created in this field and its location on earth, which was to help humans understand that everything is connected in this universe and beyond. I asked to be shown how this crop circle been created and by whom, but was not given any insight. Then a disturbance brought me out of my meditation, I opened my eyes to see that two new crop circle seekers were walking just a few feet in front of me. I stood up and explored the circle with open hands facing palm down. I wanted to pick up on the rising energies, which proved to be particularly powerful.

After about an hour, our group intuitively reconnected and we individually made our way towards the cars. There were now several other people exploring this latest circle.

On our return to the cars, I said to Kath: "Word seems to get around fast."

"Yes, it's not long before a new circle is infiltrated, which is good, the more the better. This is one way that the negative mindset towards crop circles can or is being changed. You would be surprised how many reject crop circles without having been in one."

Kath questioned others and possibly herself: "Without such an experience, how can it be judged?"

This rang true for me.

"Yes, why do people judge?"

"It's fear Ralph, they fear what they do not know or understand. The fear of there being a higher form of intelligence out there is enormous."

I understood this through the transformation of my own fears and reflected on her remarks.


The next evening Kath informed me she had a crop circle presentation at a pub, which was an hour's drive away. "Would you like to assist me? Jim usually comes with me to presentations, but on this occasion, he has some work to do and can't to attend."

"I'd be only too happy to participate."

We arrived at a pub called "The Stag" in good time for our 19.30 start. I helped carry the projector and screen along a corridor that led into a hall type room at the back of the pub. The atmosphere in the room was pleasant, and everything was set up on time. The room was filling up and just before the start of the presentation I did a quick head count, which came to forty-three

Kath's presentation of the crop circle phenomena was well orchestrated and factual. She gave a comprehensive history of crop circles which included a rich slide show.

About an hour later, Kath concluded her presentation by suggesting a short break for refreshments, after which she would be happy to answer any questions. I felt that there were many in the room who wanted to know more about crop circles and had a positive outlook, whilst some were clearly non-believers. One or two were even disrespectful and had interrupted Kath's presentation a couple of times. One had even accused her of scaremongering. Another had asked her if she was of this planet. She closed her presentation with one vital bit of advice: "Before you judge a crop circle, go into one, a real one, have the experience, then you will be better qualified to comment."

Many applauded Kath's presentation and a few left,

disgruntled. The question session that followed was a real cruncher, but it gave a clear indication that there were many more believers than non-believers. The nonbelievers' justification was based on their belief that all crop circles were man-made with planks and rollers. They chose not to accept the scientific evidence to the contrary. Kath had clearly explained that science has proven that the lower stems of crop circles have received some form of radiation producing heat that then bent the plant stems to make the formation. This heat exchange even changed the chemical compound of the stem and the earth. This raised the immediate question of *who* or *what* was creating the crop circles, to which Kath answered: "I don't really know, which is why we keep our studies open, but I am sure of one thing, the true crop circles are not man-made."

I could feel that her truth and openness touched many. For me it was a memorable evening.

I spent a further four days with Jim and Kath before heading for my next festival which was in the far north east of England. I was hitch-hiking up the east coast, above the Wash, and was dropped off at Mablethorpe in north east Lincolnshire. I bought some food from a local shop and found my way to a coastal path that gave access to the beach. The shop owner had informed me that it was a great place to be, with lots of sand dunes. The weather was still good, warm, and often hot. After my recent experiences, a question still burned in my mind. Who had created the crop circles? I decided to focus on this very question in my next meditation.

I found a suitable spot to camp for the night and set myself up. I had made a small fire and was relaxed and settled down. I went into meditation mode to remain clear of the logic. I asked the Great White Spirit how crop circles are formed. I went into a deep state of meditation and began to channel. The next thing I experienced was my astral flying through the galaxy. I stopped and found myself floating in space. I understood that I was on the outer rim of this universe. I could see the enormous curve of the Universal bubble. It was a bit like being up in the stratosphere of earth observing the curve of its aura, its protective shield. I asked my question: "Why am I here?"

Then a voice answered: *"All the information for each crop circle formation is gathered at the outer rim of this universe. Try to visualise our universe as a bubble within which our galaxy and world are held."*

From this position I could see the information that is gathered to make crop circles coming towards me; they were geometrical forms, which were a circle, hexagonal, oblong, a square, and many others.

The voice continued: *"This information is held and formalised prior to being funnelled down to earth as a ball of light to create a crop circle. The location of each crop circle is also of prime importance. Each individual area of land is specifically chosen by the higher beings because it holds the correct vibration that helps to enhance the formations. The vibration is connected to specific crystals that are hidden under the ground helping to create a vortex of energy which is connected to a specific ley line. Everything that is experienced on earth is ruled by the laws that govern this universe and galaxy; just as it is with the coded energy of a crop circles that are funnelled through to a specific sight. The light force of the crop circle makers is a highly evolved intelligence (super consciousness). The information that is gathered on the edge of this universe for a crop circle, when complete, becomes a ball of light. It then travels down to earth at a speed that is beyond comprehension and cannot be measured by logical time travel. On reaching its target – a specific crop - it stops. Remember, that quantum physics is at work here. The energy ball hovers above the crop, and in a split second the formation appears where the crop once stood. The intelligent vibration, the ball of light, which holds the crop circle information, changes the energy structure of the plant itself. It does this by manipulating the ethereal energy of each plant in a collective vibration, which forms the crop circle in a second.*

*I am sure that you have heard of the term, 'energy bends'? This is exactly what the crop circle makers do. The coded vibration bends the energy of the plant so that it can be woven and shaped into the exact coded form of the circle. Up to five different layers occur in crop circles, often laid in opposite directions from each other. By manipulating the plants structure in this manner little damage is caused to the plant itself, we are here to create, not to harm anything."*

"Yes, I do believe that the crop circle makers are a powerful but gentle force. They are here to build, not destroy. Is it true that the laws that create crop circles are within each of us as in nature; they are balancing and healing through universal laws."

*"Yes, what you think is true. Crop circles contain highly evolved forms of intelligence, and above all, they are being directed here to help humans to evolve and grow through Love and Light - the very source of all living things. Let us join hands and bend a bit*

*more, to become those bridges, to seek knowledge and wisdom from the crop circles. In this way humans may truly connect with the source of the Circles of Life."*

"It is beyond my comprehension why so much time, money and recourses are spent on looking for intelligent forms out there in the universe, when in fact it is already occurring here and now on earth. But is that a reflection or a fault of the human mind and its nature? What are your thoughts on this?"

*"I will simply say that humanity, more often, believes that the answers to life are outside and are to be found somewhere else."*

Another vision came into my mind's eye. I was standing in the middle of a medieval castle. It was summertime and I was almost overwhelmed by the perfume of roses. I spotted a billboard by the side of a stone stairway stating "Art Exhibition Upstairs". I instantly felt a positive impulse to make my way up the steps to the open door at the top. I entered the doorway, stepping out of sunlight into a more subdued setting of shadowy coolness. I stood there for a few moments to get my bearings. Some ten yards or more to my right, there stood a small table behind which sat an African man. He wore a silky green and gold kaftan type dress. Perhaps he was the artist.

We made eye contact and acknowledged each other with a warm smile. I turned to my right to view the first picture, which I believed to have been painted by the man sitting at the table. I folded my arms across my chest and held my right hand under my chin whilst I gazed and assessed the oil painting in front of me. I knew there was something familiar about the painting but had, at that point, not grasped its full meaning.

After some minutes I moved along to the next painting. Once again, I stood some five paces back to study the artwork. Then there came a "Eureka" moment. I had a flashback to the moment when in outer space, I watched the geometric forms coming out of the cosmic abyss towards me. In the picture on the wall, as with all the rest of his collection, the artist had painted one oblong on top of the other to create a street scene. The colours were strong and pronounced, making the painting vibrant and alive. There were layers upon layers of slightly differing colours and tones that gave the picture life. I knew that the artist, realised or unrealised, was channelling his gift through his higher consciousness as art. His artwork was connected to the geometrical form that came through his soul vibration. His soul was then able to express itself through his artwork, giving incalculable pleasure to others. This was the human connection to the crop circles, they are geometrical!

Now I had the complete, or at least, a strong sense of how, why and in what ways we are being influenced by forces beyond our imagination. All the pieces fit together after that moment. I was indeed blessed by the experience.

I had another question: "Which higher beings create the crop circles? Is it the Vitrumai of Stonehenge or the Salasiani; the pyramid builders from Swz?"

There was a long pause before I received anything, and then came the reply: *"The creators of crop circles belong to neither of these. Their home is in the sixth universe in the 1,300-galaxy known as Tupai. Their world is several times larger than Earth."*

"What is their world called?"

*"Wait a minute, I have to check that one out."*

After a long pause there came a reply: *"They are a bit cautious about who they share their knowledge with. Their world is called Andorinu. The Welsh translation is 'heddychol' or in English 'peaceful'. They tell me that they always seek to harmonise energies, and they seem to know of you."*

"How do they know me?"

*"They are telling me that you have visited their world in your sleep state, because like them you are also here to serve the earth people for the greater good. They send you their greetings."*

I was surprised by what I had been told. I reflected upon its ramifications. Thoughts came flooding into my mind. Did I want to know more? The answer came quickly. Yes, I did.

"How am I going to serve others?"

*"You are already doing it by learning to embrace not fight your experiences on earth. Every experience you now have is raising your consciousness because your thoughts and actions are primarily spiritually based. Look deeper within, for there is a well of knowledge there."*

"So why here? Why Earth? Why create crop circles when I am sure you could simply visit and appear to the human eye. This would surely sort out the many doubters and sceptics."

*"They tell me that the mystical side creates greater curiosity which helps to raise the consciousness of many. It helps people to look for other solutions or insights into the crop circle phenomena, and that is healthy for the human psyche. You are living proof that it's working. Besides if we were to visit, as you put it, it would scare many, particularly those who are meant to protect your nations from enemy forces. However, we are not your enemy, far from it. We have no fear of anything, unlike the human's logic, your weapons, any weapons are like, as you say in English 'water off a duck's back'. We are not threatened by them, they are harmless to us."*

"From historical records it seems that the crop circles have been created on earth for over 15,000 years. Why wait so long?"

*"They now want to speak to you directly Ralph. Let's see how it flows."*

"Good, I believe I am ready."

*"Ralph, this is a special moment for both of us. We share our joy with you, and now for some further insight. Our main message for earth people is that we are already here. You need not search further. We can help you evolve beyond the stage that you are passing through now, more quickly, by the correct approach and use of mind. The human being's evolutionary process from being ego centric to higher mind orientation, i.e. soul expression, has been very slow and painful. But we the Andorinu people who, by the way, are known as Malinutru, are peace loving higher beings whose technology is supreme. We are one of several caretakers of universal laws through which the earth was created. The ego is a*

*false energy that was implanted in some of the human's logical consciousness by alien beings many thousands of years ago with the agenda to control the earth beings."*

"Wow that's intense. I must process that one. So, you are solely responsible for creating the crop circles?"

*"The forces are already there. We are simply a channel for their creation, just like you are now being used to share this insight with others. It's a means and not an end, as some believe and some do not."*

"So, what does the circle I was in yesterday represent?"

*"It was created to help establish a greater vibration of peace on earth."*

"How does that work in little Wiltshire?"

*"From the moment the crop circle is created, it emanates its vibration back out into the Matrix of universal consciousness. It is then able to draw upon the entire universal life force, which you felt, even before you physically walked into the circle. This is helping to strengthen the magnetic shield that surrounds earth whilst at the same time negate any negative forces in the entire region."*

"That's true, I did feel different. The energy was strong but calm at the same time. Tell me, is there a great cover-up regarding you, the Andorinu people, from various governments?"

*"There is, but the knowledge they have is very limited due to the way it's been approached. Fear creates a strong repulsion of the truth that appears in crop circles and other forms of communication. These are*

*the ego and fear, which are the two main forces that are preventing humans from evolving. They hold the psyche in the 3D. The ego detests something it cannot control or understand. Our own mother ship is not far from earth, it's been there, undetected for many a decade."*

"How is that? I mean why can't we see you? Is our radar too dense in its application?"

*"Yes, it is. We are masters of disguise. The negative aliens are also unable to detect us due to the advanced technology we use, otherwise, we would not have survived their attacks."*

"Others? You mean that there are extremely negative aliens out there?"

*"Oh yes. Thus far, we the Malinutru, have eluded the Zakrav aliens. We have engaged with them in many a galactic war, but they have not been able to penetrate our shields."*

"Well, I'm really grateful for all that you have done for earth and its people, as I am certain others would be, including the military establishments of the various nations. So what is going to take place next?"

*"In one respect, it's up to the human consciousness in relation to the choices made and action taken that determines your outcome. What would be a positive step forward would be if all government leaders stopped fearing us and all sciences would come together to collectively recognise, or in some cases admit, that higher beings exist within this galaxy in one form or another. As soon as their consciousness allows them to admit this fact, then the higher beings that are waiting to communicate, will come to*

*share some of their higher technology. Without this, little change will take place, possibly for a number of decades. To date, the research that has been done on crop circles (by ethical groups with true intentions), has been accurately depicted through the circles geometrical alignments, giving an accurate account of certain planetary and galactic systems. Many are linked to what has been enacted and depicted in many of the Shamanic cultures throughout the world. So, it's not that the human race does not know. Many choose not to remember or open the doors to their inner knowing."*

"Okay, so fear is yet again responsible for much of the negative approach taken towards the crop circle phenomena."

*"Yes and no. Fear is there but so is the Ego and the vested interests of politicians connected to it. That's part of the illusion that has been created by those who choose not to accept, or those that know, but will not admit it. What is now occurring in relation to this is much, much bigger. We will not fully appear at present because the action taken by the military would have disastrous effects on humans and Earth itself. We are here to help and protect the world from a strong negative alien force that are void of the Love Ray. They have not evolved through the Love Ray as all humans and higher beings have."*

"Wait a moment, Love Ray? What's that?"

*"The Love Ray is the light source of your creator God. You are a seed of that ray; you are everything that God is, which is what makes humans unique. Your body type is a miracle, a creation of how God's love can be expressed through others. This is why it has*

*attracted so much universal attention.”*

“But if this is true, why is there so much negativity being expressed in all walks of life, on all continents?”

*“To put it simply the transformation of the ego is of key importance; it controls much of what has taken place on earth for thousands of years. It is the implant I talked about earlier. There are now major changes taking place by those who are waking up - raising their consciousness - to the hold that the ego has over global consciousness. There is a healthy counter-revolution, an uprising of consciousness that is connected to the matrix of God consciousness, and this will not fail.”*

“I am so very happy to hear that, it warms my heart.”

*“Good, now we understand each other and have become closer.”*

I felt the connection was fading and I thanked my guide and other higher beings for the insights given and I slowly came back to earth. For some moments it seemed strange to be feeling the physical body gain. The sound and feel of the ocean helped to ground me further. I checked my watch; I had been gone for almost three hours, but it felt like five minutes. The time lapse, although not logically understood, helped to confirm that there were different time zones associated with higher and lower levels of consciousness. I had a peaceful, deep night’s sleep on the beach. Ever since that time I refer to crop circles as **Circles of Life.**

# Chapter 8

# Angel Beings

These last four years of my life were rich in spiritual experiences. I had not crashed or lost myself in my spiritual development. The gradual transformation of my consciousness from 3D orientation into 4D was gaining strength. I was living life more and more in the present moment. This was a sure sign that higher consciousness was being actively applied in my life.

In the mid-summer of 1992, I had a profound experience of Kundalini rising[13] that transformed my emotional body. I was assisting Angela, a spiritual teacher, to read the energies of the students that were attending a course of hers in Czechoslovakia. My three higher senses had been in full flow for over a year and I had developed my own technique for applying them. I had learnt to use my higher senses only when applicable and with respect. After a morning session, I went to rest in my room. I lay on my bed and closed my eyes to contemplate what had taken place. I drifted off into a semi-unconscious state. I felt a strong light energy filling my whole being. A picture of my seven chakras appeared in my mind's eye. I started to shiver, which became more violent. I could no longer feel my physi-

---

13 Kundalini rising is the life force – light – that is represented as fire, of which there are three, i.e. physical, electromagnetic and atomic, which flows downwards, passing through each chakra to rise again. As the kundalini rises it burns away the old energy, such as feelings and thoughts that are blocking or hindering one's spiritual development. The kundalini is a purification of one's energies.

cal body, yet I knew it was there. A burning sensation filled my first chakra, the root chakra. A shivering cold feeling appeared and disappeared on three occasions in a matter of minutes. I could feel the strong energy moving upwards from the first chakra into the second, the sacral. I was starting to sweat profusely. There was a strong sense of pain from within the sacral chakra. I focused my thoughts on the heat of the energy and began to breathe through it. No effect, in fact the heat intensified. I then understood that this was a strong kundalini experience taking place within me and I needed to follow its path with complete willingness.

The pain grew more intense within my second chakra. I was now rolling in pain. I again focused on my breathing and started to change it from quick shallow breaths to long deep ones, and stayed focused on the second chakra. I visualised the energy of the chakra and saw there were some green and red colours flowing through it. The colours were slowly being transformed into pure light. In a previous experience of consciousness rising through the chakras, I had come to understand that any colour within the chakras was in fact a block of the energy flow, which was important to transform into light, colour is a lower vibration of light.

Some four hours later the kundalini energy had continued rising from my first chakra into the second and was now passing into the third. I felt a strong resistance in the third chakra, so I focused more deeply on the sacral and used the breath to breathe through that chakra to allow the rise into the third chakra unimpeded. After many breaths I felt the energy begin to move upwards. The burning pain began to ease, and I relaxed a little. I lay there holding the transforming force for some time; whether it was four hours or more I could not tell. Then the pain began to intensify as another wave of energy swept through the second chakra into the third. I remained focused on these two charkas and realised that I had some unresolved issues related to both chakras and began to work more deeply on them.

Again, I used the breath to help the energy flow. Pictures and emotions appeared which gave me insight into where I had not transformed the energies within these two chakras. My whole body became hotter; it felt like I was literally burning up. I started to physically shake again. I understood that the shaking was due to the central nervous system being refreshed (for want of a word), it was taking away the old cellular memories.

The pain again intensified, it was not over, and I was determined not to block this natural flow of energy. In that moment I surrendered unconditionally to the kundalini force and let go of my conditioning and fears related to the three lower chakras. As soon as I had decided not to fight it, but to go with its flow, there was a sudden shift of energy. A strong release of something deep within occurred. I felt the resistance between the second and third chakra had faded away and my third chakra was being filled with the warm energy of the kundalini.

I remained focused on this transformation, which I believe was for one or more hours. I continued to apply my breath with the colours that appeared to help the flow of the kundalini. The pain began to ease dramatically as the energy began to move from the third chakra up into the fourth, the heart chakra. A deep sense of peace filled my whole being, I felt at one with myself and the universe.

I began to wake up and found myself in a dimly lit room which had only moments ago been full of light. The summer clothes I had on were completely soaked with my perspiration. I looked at the clock on the wall it was 8 p.m. I had been away for some seven hours and I had missed the afternoon session. I was too exhausted by the experience to move. I decided not to go to supper and with some effort, I managed to take off my damp clothes. I rested under a single sheet and fell into a deep sleep.

I was woken by a knock on the door. "Come on in", I said and the course leader Angela came in.

She said in her broken English: "Are you all right Ralph? I felt that I should not send someone to look for you yesterday afternoon when you didn't show up or to disturb you last night."

"Yes, thanks for that, you must have been tuned into me. I have been through a strong kundalini experience and I needed to rest after, for it to settle down, but I'm ok now."

"Good, breakfast is ready in thirty minutes, are you coming down?"

"Oh yes, we can discuss the day's programme then."

"See you shortly."

Three weeks later I returned to Wales from central Europe. It was late summer and was about to embark on another trip, this time, to Thailand. I had booked a flight at Stansted airport for Monday leaving at 6.45 p.m. I left a friend's house in Pembrokeshire at 8 a.m. and walked to the main road with my home on my back, my rucksack. I started to hitchhike to London and then on to Stansted airport, which was about a six-hour drive. After about thirty minutes I got a lift to another main road that led to the motorway. I was dropped off in a bad spot and walked for twenty minutes or so to a more favourable place where cars could stop. The weather was good, but lifts were slow in coming. An hour passed, still in the same place. I realised that I may have miscalculated the time for my trip to London. In the next moment, a box lorry pulled over.

I rushed over to open the door.

"Jump in mate", shouted the driver over the noise of cars rushing past like an endless mechanical steam train.

I plonked myself onto the two-person seat and the driver pushed the gearstick forward, gave me a wink and we rushed off.

"Where are you heading for mate?"

"London", I responded.

"Ah good, I can take you right up to the M25, should be alright from there."

"Great".

He threw out the butt of a cigarette he had in his mouth and offered me one before he lit another.

"No thanks I don't smoke."

"Good for you, wish I could say the same. My name is Mike by the way."

Waving my left hand I said: "Hi, my name's Ralph. Thanks for the lift. I'm going to Stansted, then Thailand for a few months."

"Wish I could come with you. I'll drop you off at a roundabout where you can get a lift to Stansted."

"Great, thanks", I replied.

The lorry was empty and our progress good until we got to the outskirts of the M25, London's circular road, which was notorious for congestion. Mike dropped me off at what he thought was a good spot, but in a matter of minutes I realised that he had probably never hitch-hiked anywhere before, let alone at this spot. There was no room for a car to pull over let alone stop. The cars that passed were ferocious, all speeding along; everyone seemed to be in a mad rush to get to some-where. It was 3.30 p.m. and time was running short. An hour or so had passed; one car attempted to stop, but quickly moved on as horns blared and the flow of cars psychically pursued him. I could feel the aggression of the drivers. It seemed like madness; they were possessed by time. With no sign of a lift, I decided that I needed some help and put a thought out to Great White Spirit.

Some fifteen minutes later an old broken-down car slowly passed me, which immediately caught my attention. The driver looked sideways and up at me. The car indicator was on and it pulled in a hundred yards down the slip road that led onto the M25. I grabbed my rucksack, ran for the car, opened the back door, threw my rucksack onto the back seat, and jumped in. The male driver simply smiled at me in a warm manner and drove off. There was a stillness in the car that I had not often experienced. It was as if I, or we, were cocooned; no it felt like a time capsule. We were in motion, but it did not feel real, it was surreal. We seemed to be travelling but there was no sound, no direct interaction with the road, traffic, or anything else. I closed my eyes, took a deep breath, and thanked Heaven for this lift. I looked at the driver who seemed to be normal on the outside, but I detected a faint glow coming from his skin, a kind of effervescence. This effect blurred the edges of his appearance.

Several minutes must have passed before the driver asked me where I was going. I said Stansted airport, and he looked at me, still holding his smile.

"It's a bit late to get there by car now."

"You're probably right. Where are you going to?"

"Nowhere special", he replied.

Then a deeper moment's pause filled the car. Suddenly, he swerved off the M25 onto a slip road.

"I'll take you to the railway station just up the road here; you can get the next direct train to Stansted. It's ok, you have five minutes to catch the train."

I noticed that he was not wearing a watch; nor was

there one in the car, an old 1969 Austin 1300. In those few seconds, I realised that this man was not of this planet. There was an aura about him that was calm, collected and assuring. Sure enough, within the next minute or two we pulled up outside the train station. We did not even shake hands, he simply smiled back at me just as he had done when he pulled over to give me a lift, some ten minutes earlier. I got out and thanked him for the lift and bid him goodbye.

He replied in his calm manner: "Have a good trip and keep doing whatever it is your doing."

Then he drove off. I made the flight, and knew that on some level, I had received divine intervention from an Angel.

Some six months later I met a deeply spiritual woman called Lora. We were discussing and exploring the Angelic realms. I shared with her my experience of having a lift from what I believe was an angel.

When I had finished sharing, Lora said: "That's very interesting Ralph, I too believe that there is such a thing as divine intervention. I would like to share a similar experience, which I had only last month."

I nodded in agreement.

There was a moment's pause and then Lora began: "I was on my way to give a presentation on the West coast of America. I was driving along in the middle of the prairies when my car broke down. There was no house in sight, only hills and more hills and a long, long road. I raised the bonnet of the car and clouds of steam came pouring out, which quickly rose and evaporated in the heat of the day. I stood there for a moment wondering what to do next. I looked up and down the road, which seemed to go for miles in either direction; not a car in sight. I leaned against the passenger's door and looked across the plains. It was hot, and I had a small bottle of water but no food. I thought to myself this does not look good. I needed help.

Some moments later my attention was drawn to some bushes in the far distance. I saw someone walking, and they were walking towards me. As they came closer I could tell that it was a man, wearing mechanic overalls and he was carrying a toolbox. I wondered who he might be. As he came closer, it seemed to me he was walking effortlessly. You know when you walk on semi desert it can be very sandy, and this area was, but it was as if he was not influenced by gravity.

He came up to the car, gave me a smile and began to work on the engine. He did not utter one word to me. I was glued to the spot. There were no sounds made as he worked on the engine, he seemed to be touching things, but to me nothing major was done. He looked across to me and just gave an enigmatic smile, just like the one you experienced six months ago. In a matter of minutes, he closed his toolbox, closed the bonnet of the car, turned to smile at me again and walked off in the direction he came from. Not a word had been spoken. It felt like I was in a trance. Was this real? I pinched myself, took a drink of water and sat in the car. Some moments later, how long, I do not know, I turned the ignition key and as true as I am sitting here today, the engine started. It goes without saying, I made the presentation in plenty of time."

Upon hearing Lora's personal story, I knew that Spirit works on many planes and can be anywhere in any form, whenever the intentions are pure of heart and mind. A couple of weeks had passed, and I felt that I needed a meditation to obtain deeper insights into the Angelic world. I settled down and soon went into a transitional state of meditation.

I travelled to the meeting place where I could be with

my main guide to seek council.

"Hello, I am happy to be with you again."

*"This is also true for me. I can see that you have something on your mind."*

"Well yes, I do. Can you share some of your knowledge of how the Angel Realm works?"

*"Of course, but it's a vast area to cover. You must be a bit more specific than that. Remember, to get the right answer you must ask the right question."*

"Let me rephrase. Are there different levels on the Angelic realm? You know there is a class system on earth, which is not talked about these days. I know there are seven Archangels, but what about other angel types?"

*"I can see what prompts your line of thought, and you are quite right to enquire. There is a sense of order in the spiritual realms, a hierarchy that is not politically based or determined by how much money one earns or possessions one has. There are many levels of Angel beings. As it is with all forms of beings, it is the amount of light that is held within its energy that determines how evolved a being is. It's a matter of applied intelligence and heart presence. There are apprentice Angels in Heaven just as there are apprentice carpenters on earth. Everything in this and other universes are evolving and initiating, just as you are on earth."*

"I have seen pictures of angel babies in books and paintings. Are there really, baby Angels?"

*"Yes, there are, but a few words of advice. Don't mix rational logic with higher thought. Everything is possible on a spiritual realm. As you have already experienced, physical laws are extremely limited, which is simply due to the light frequency of the sun, your star. There are many steps to climb and master on the physical plane before you even reach the first step of the Divine Order, which is being a spiritual helper, let alone an angel."*

"What is a spiritual helper?"

*"A spiritual helper is a soul that has mastered their physical life by raising their consciousness into the fifth dimension and above, whereby all chakras are united as one force; meaning that they hold no fear and feel from their heart, not through emotions. They are fully present. Every moment is like a walking meditation and as such, is fully enlightened with no need to return to the physical plane to serve. Some decide to return, often remaining anonymous to those who are unaware of the love and light they hold. In other words, their life is lived without a shadow, which is where you want to be, right?"*

"Oh yes, for sure. I am certain you are aware of my endeavours in that area. So, the guy who picked me up the day I was flying to Thailand, was making sure that I would not miss my flight. Was he an angel or a guide?"

*"Let's take one thing at a time. Only Archangels can actively participate in what is referred to as Divine Intervention. Divine intervention occurs when a higher being such as an Archangel changes or at times holds the circumstances for the greater good,*

*which is not a common happening. For example, you were given a lift at exactly the right moment to stop you getting into harm's way. Deep within you, you felt when that moment came to you; take yourself back to when you had a bad feeling when you were stuck on that dangerous roundabout of the M25."*

I pondered for a few moments on what he had been saying. "You're right. I did have a strong negative feeling for some minutes and was trying to work it out. I thought it was just the bad vibes of the drivers. You know it's easy to get lost in the mind games. So, was I in imminent danger?"

*"Yes you were. Many light workers, like yourself, are taken out or killed by dark forces under the disguise of accidents. Always remember, there is no such thing as an accident, there's a happening."*

"I have an important question regarding those moments. What would have happened if I had not asked for help form Spirit?"

*"We, or rather the angel being, could not have interfered with your decision making, but fortunately you were listening and felt the negative force coming, which unconsciously prompted you to seek help. So, the lesson of the day, is to keep on listening to your intuition. But be aware, this law is not to be abused or used incorrectly; it cannot operate under false apprehensions or wishes, such as wishing for material gain."*

"Okay, I understand and I am so grateful for the divine intervention. So, what is the next evolutionary step on this spiritual path into Heaven?"

*"Are you referring to yourself?"*

"Yes, and no. Well firstly, being a spiritual helper on the Heavenly plane?"

*"It warms my heart to hear that you so readily put others before you. All spiritual helpers decide where to serve, be it on the earth plane or from a heavenly body. Spiritual helpers do not hold the same energy as main guides do. They are not connected to any specific soul; they are free to be anywhere. For example, when you are giving spiritual healing you have at times asked for help and a Chinese doctor appeared. You then stepped back to allow his specialised healing to blend with your patient's energies and you were totally trusting of this doctor. This Chinese doctor assists many healers if called on, your mother included, when she was on the earth plane. For the Chinese Doctor it's like going from one hospital to another and he can also be in two or more places at once."*

"Oh, so you know of my spiritual helper. I now understand, but I have been visited by more than one spirit helper for my healing work. How is that?"

*"Because it's what you require. It's not that your healing doesn't work, it's quite the opposite. You may need some assistance at times; so spirit healers come to assist you and many others from the above, or as it is often referred to, Heaven."*

"I now know what to call them; they are floating helpers."

*"That works!"*

"So, in the spiritual hierarchy, who comes next?"

*"The next level of servers are main guides like me, of which there are two forms. The first, are guides that are connected to a single person and will remain to help and guide the individual until the fifth plane of consciousness is established. The second, is a guide that someone is channelling to give insight to others, such as in groups or deeper spiritual courses. White Eagle is one of the better known Guides that are serving from this high plane of consciousness. The main guide is followed by angels, then the seven masters, and God."*

"Wow, there's a long way for me to go!"

*"It's not as far away as you might believe; you are now firmly on your spiritual path. You know that there is only one way you can go and that is forward and upwards. You are already putting this into practice by not living in the past or the future. You now know that way of applying one's consciousness simply keeps you locked into the illusions of the past, where ego and fear can control and consume you. Every positive thought, every positive action is lifting your psyche towards enlightenment. Every spiritual helper, guide, angel, and master have experienced everything that you have. All spiritual beings, on whichever level, have evolved from experiences, just like you are now doing. One cannot master life unless all aspects have been experienced and mentally understood, which includes higher consciousness. How else can it be? All negative energies must be transformed."*

"Well yes, I do see the wisdom behind it. Is this part of

The Greater Plan that I hear people talk of?"

*"Ah yes, The Greater Plan. We are both participating in The Greater Plan, which is to enlighten global consciousness. The earth is a living body of energy; it has feelings just like you do. When it is irritated or has an itch, it will move to relieve itself, this is partly why earthquakes occur. Nature expresses the mood of the world you live in; everything is vibration and is connected."*

"I can really feel what you are saying is true. Does that mean that the world has a consciousness?"

*"Oh yes, and what's more, you are taking an increasingly active part in its expansion. Let me put it like this. You are a universe within a universe, and at present you are on earth, a living organism, an embodiment of spirit and soul, a divine being. Just like all living beings you have a consciousness that is connected to the matrix of universal consciousness. This is what energy is. It's a bit like this, your spinal cord is connected to your control area; your consciousness, not the brain. The brain does not think, it is a receiver and sender of consciousness. Your consciousness is connected to the God source through your soul cord that flows through your crown chakra, which in turn unites and maintains the life force of the dense physical body. In your brain there are billions of neurons that help maintain your physical and spiritual life force. Now expand your thoughts, and imagine the earth as a brain, and that you are one of those neurons that are holding a positive light force.*

*Here is the magical bit. Every person that you touch*

*with your light, you will awaken something within them, and that awakening may take them to follow a spiritual path, just like you. Eventually they will touch another to follow spiritual laws of truth, love, joy, and peace. This is how love and light will reach others through humans taking an active role in it. There are some 8 billion humans of Earth and each one is connected to the matrix, which creates global consciousness, which in turn is held within universal consciousness. There are many dark areas on Earth, many shadows to transform and enlighten. You and millions of others like you, are serving and reaching out to touch the negative and the shadows to transform them. The world is being transformed in this manner. Eventually there will be more light beings on earth than dark, and the dark side will no longer be able to hide behind the ego or fear because it will no longer overshadow the psyche of individuals and the collective. This is the ultimate goal of The Greater Plan; to have an enlightened world."*

"That's amazing, I feel like jumping with joy."

*"Please do!"*

"What will happen to the earth and all its inhabitants once global consciousness is fulfilled?"

*"Peace on Earth will once again be established."*

"You mean it's been here before?"

*"Yes, it has, that was some 300,000 years ago just after the big freeze when the migration of the three races of people became more unified. The consciousness of the region grew to create the Atlantis expe-*

*rience where life was in harmony with nature, and the laws of the universe were being applied for the greater good. The consciousness of the Atlantean people continued to rise until 20,000 B.C. when it became corrupt by the ego, and the dark side took over the alien human nature. The Earth felt this, and a cleansing took place. A great majority of the souls from that period have been reincarnating to transform the negative aspects of their innate nature through DNA transformation. The nature of the dark side has not changed over millennia, but humans are now held in a deep transition, as the Earth receives a higher frequency of light. This light frequency will assist in the changes required in the DNA of many millions of people whose DNA received the implanted alien ego. But not all people's DNA on earth were corrupted. Many millions more are clear; these are the souls that are at the forefront of transforming the ego."*

"Wow that's an amazing insight. I have never heard anyone talk about this. To me it often does not seem like that, there is so much destruction and war mongering taking place all over the world. To me it seems the opposite is happening."

*"You seem to be confused. Let's take one question at a time. First, as Earth receives more light, it is helping to raise consciousness. Second, the destruction has always been there but seems more because the awareness of it has increased dramatically in the last decade. Social media is a very positive development on one level, but it is important to observe one's judgment of events. The dark side will only show its own favourable side to implement its own agenda. The light, however, cannot hide anything,*

*all is to be seen, no hidden agenda. The dark side in one respect seems to have grown in strength because it is fighting itself out of a corner. It's losing its identity, it needs to be seen and recognised. The light side does not require identity because it already IS! It has nothing to prove, simply to be!"*

"When will all of this madness end, you know, the killing, the judgment, the jealousy and envy?"

*"Many masters and Angels have come to earth to share universal truth, to spread the word amongst the peoples, but did they listen to Jesus, Gandhi, Martin Luther King and many other light workers? Some did, the greater majority not. None the less the seeds were planted then, and these are now beginning to bear fruit. The spirit within all humans cannot be controlled or trapped for too long, it will eventually break the chains of suppression and control as is now being witnessed globally."*

"What part can I play in this, how can I be of greater help?"

*"You are exactly where you are meant to be in every moment of your life. Continue to listen to your inner calling, follow your intuition, be true to the self and above all love the self. All else will follow; you need not look for anything outside of yourself because everything is within and will therefore come to you. The answers are within."*

"I am practicing being present and following spiritual practices, and I do feel the wellbeing you talk about. Is there anything else I should be doing to help my spiritual development?"

*"Simply follow your heart in whatever you do, that's where peace resides, being true to yourself!"*

"I feel blessed to have you as my guide, your wisdom and insight have been invaluable. It feels as if I am beginning to see the world through your eyes now. Is that true?"

*"Yes, that is an important part of your spiritual soul transformation. It's a strong indication that your higher senses are functioning correctly. You are me and I am you, this is a definition of 'oneness'."*

"There you go again, your wisdom shines through. I will endeavour to follow your wishes."

*"You don't have to try, just be. The universe demands nothing of you. One of your earthly expressions is to 'keep on keeping on'. This is good for you; don't let any negative thought take hold. You remember when you were stood in a large football stadium when you were seven years old with your brother. You were with your grandfather who had come to listen to a political leader. He left you for a few moments and when he returned two large men had pushed you out of your seats. Well as small as your grandfather was, he spoke with the power of truth to the two large men that had treated you in such an egotistical manner. You could see them shrink as your grandfather boldly showed them their disgraceful behaviour towards two little boys. This is the truth and the power I talk about, not being afraid of what others may think. Be true to your heart and continue to grow."*

"That is true. I have often thought of my grandfather

when I was looking for strength to pass through something. He really has been a source of strength and inspiration for me. Well now I understand that there really is no separation, he must have been with me in spirit, in such difficult times."

*"Yes, he was. I'm sure you now understand how truth love and light are eternal forces of energy."*

"Wow, yes, I do. Wow! Hmm, one last thing comes to mind. You very briefly mentioned Heaven. What is Heaven? I often felt that my Grandfather and other loved ones are in Heaven, but is it a world, a special place where only the good guys go?"

*"That's an important question. I will endeavour to explain your question in two ways that lead to the same truth. Directly, Heaven is universal consciousness. Indirectly, Heaven is created wherever the values of love, light, truth and joy are lived by. It can be on a planet, galaxy or even, an entire universe. It is not a place that is outside of you, it is within, and you are the creative source, the seed of light, and the heavenly body. I will step back for now brother Ralph, God speed!"*

I felt my guide withdrawing from my vibration and fading away into the light. I gradually returned to full body awareness and rested for some time. It was important to absorb every word and feeling I had received from my main guide. Eventually I got up and made myself a cup of tea, which was always good for grounding my energies, black tea was indeed my earthing. The deep conversation I had with my main guide was still racing through my head and body. I started to analyse what we shared from a logical perspective, which I felt was important because I was educating the left hemisphere to accept the realities of higher-minded principles.

# Chapter 9

## Eternity

I decided to take a walk in nature and called Mark to see if he wanted to join me. Nearly two weeks had passed since our last meeting. An hour later we met at one of our favourite spots in a gorge that was deeply forested. It was a place where we had taken walks on many occasions, and as we ambled along, I felt that we had entered a meditative state. The sunlight was pouring through the thick trees, which were mostly pine and spruce, but along this stretch of the path there were also some enormous ancient oak trees. Birds were singing and I noticed that a Buzzard was soaring above us, which for me was a sure sign that Spirit was with us. Life was rich, what a blessing to be here. I felt that Mark sensed that I was processing something and he asked: "Is everything alright Ralph?"

"What do you think about angels?" I asked. "How real are they for you?"

"To my understanding, angels are highly evolved beings, there's no doubt about that. I believe in them."

"I'm happy to hear it", I replied.

"What brings this up for you Ralph."

"I received some deep insight about them a few weeks ago, when I was channelling."

"Ok, do you want to share something?"

"Yes, I do, and it's related to angels. I was searching for something deep to see if there was anything I may have missed during my channelling with my guide. Then it came to me. Why is it that the church always seems to emphasise the importance of angels?”

“Not sure what you mean Ralph?”

I continued to contemplate on the this question. Then an insight came to me: “I know, maybe it’s because angels are seen as protectors, you know, your guardian angel is looking over you, or is protecting you, that kind of thing.”

“I believe that is true. I certainly have asked for help on a number of occasions, and it worked for me in one way or another. For me, angels are higher beings that can and do prevent the Devil’s work. Ask for an angel’s protection and it is given, it’s as simple as that for me.”

A few moments passed before I continued: “You know, there are the seven Archangels? Michael is the Angel of Protection, Raphael is the Angel of Healing and Gabriel told Mary that she was to give birth to the baby Jesus. Uriel is the Angel of Peace and there are many others that are serving God.”

“That’s fine Ralph, glad to know that we are on the same path together, spirit brother.”

Joyously we continued our walk, through nature. The stillness of the ravine was wonderful, and we were now descending towards the small stream that had created the gorge over millennia. I realised it must be that we are evolving as angel beings, because wherever there is love there is the Divine, and the God essence also. I smiled inwardly and put my arm around my spirit brother’s shoulders to hug him as we walked along.

We held our own space for the next few hours, simply listening to the sounds of nature, breathing the rich air, washing our feet in the cool stream, and we had the fire element, the sun. I reflected how stillness and peace are to be treasured in this mad world of action and doing, doing, doing. But this was my journey, I create my own reality. I could have stayed there forever. I leaned back from where I was resting against a tree trunk and asked Mark: "What is forever?"

He closed his eyes for a few minutes to be focused. I could tell that he was channelling for clarity in his reply. I waited and stayed focused on the question I had posed Mark. He opened his eyes, took his bearings, shuffled his body, and then he was back: "Hm, that's a deep question Ralph. What happened to you this morning? You are going into things much deeper than usual."

"Well, I have this passion to go deeper; I feel there is so much I do not understand about myself, esoteric science, and the universe."

It was getting late, the sun had disappeared behind the tall trees and it had become cooler, but Mark remained focused.

"Here is my understanding of your question about the nature of forever. There is no such thing, because we are eternal beings, so how could there possibly be a forever, we are forever."

"That's a positive way to look at it. I never thought of it that way before."

There was a pause, and I felt that Mark was far from finished; I looked at him and asked him to continue.

"You're getting to know me too well Ralph, are you now reading my mind or something?"

I gave him a big smile: "Come on, tell me what you have."

"Well ..."

"Come on, stop being modest, I am keen to hear what you have been told and shown."

"The word 'forever' is a logical perception of time, and time was created to give humans a certain amount of order and structure to their lives. So, when someone uses the word forever, eternal, or everlasting, what they really mean, is infinity. Logic does not really understand the true meaning of 'forever' because anything that stands outside of the physical timeline,[14] it simply cannot be comprehended. The earth is the only place in the universe that is governed, or should I say ruled by time. In one sense eternity is everywhere else but here. For example, humans are eternal when they sleep, because the soul journeys back to its home, to another world, another galaxy or even universe. It returns when we wake up in the morning to find ourselves back in "kindergarden or school. This is a learning place, a world to evolve through spiritual values, that's the only reason we come to Earth."

"If I understand you correctly, the consciousness of logic is what operates here on Earth."

"Yes, that's correct, but more importantly logic finds it extremely difficult or impossible to imagine another reality outside of the physical timeline. For example, when the word 'Heaven' is used, it is believed to be out there in the universe somewhere, of another world, another place. I do not see it like that. Heaven is within, but few realise this fact. For me it's a matter of perception, how you view life, your left or right brain orientation."

"Let me ask you, then, when I am away from the gravitational pull of the earth and heading beyond its vibration of light, I become eternal?"

"Yes, that is true. Here is how I understand it to work; a bit of quantum physics here perhaps. Physical light is the lowest vibration of light in the universe. The physical body is the lowest density. We were created like that so that our cellular structure does not burn out. Physical light speed is approximately 670 616 629.2 miles per hour, right?"

"Right."

---

14 Physical timeline gives meaning to past present and future, time, and distance. The physical timeline is ruled by the speed of physical light in relation to the spin of the earth, which give the night and day, days, weeks, and months.

"The closer I get to that speed the shorter time becomes. So, when I go beyond the physical timeline, I am in timeless space. This for me explains why, when I have been in a deep meditation and far away astral travelling to another dimension, on my return, I look at the clock and find that I have been away for a couple of hours, when in fact it felt like a couple of minutes. I must have been way beyond the physical timeline."

There was another deep pause, before Mark continued: "So, to get back to the original point of everlasting, the physical body's lifespan is limited by the physical timeline, whereas your soul is eternal. Why? It's because the soul is not touched by the lower vibration of physical timeline when on Earth or anywhere else for that matter. It is above the physical vibration of friction, the fire of friction."

"Fantastic Mark, that was enlightening."

We sat there for ages debating eternity and the relevance of time. I understood that I needed to study physics and quantum physics to understand where the sciences were with this, were they in touch with esoteric science or not. I went back to Mark's place and stayed the night. It had been an interesting day, providing much to contemplate upon.

We continued our discussion over dinner, then sat by the open fire in silence. I rested my eyes by looking into the fire. I felt that there was something primeval about fire gazing; it took me back to somewhere deep within. I then consciously focused to see the elemental spirit of fire within the fire. In a matter of moments, I could see the fire spirits dancing in-between red, yellow and blue flames.

"I can see the fire spirits Mark, take a look."

"Oh yes, happy little things, aren't they? All elements have spirits, it's partly how the earth, air, water and fire speak through our psyche. They can even wake us up, you know Ralph, they help raise your energies."

"You're right. That's why it's so important to be in touch with nature, it nourishes us through our senses."

Then a memory came back to me and I went on: "Do you recall the night we went to a Universal Peace dance at the local hall in Nevern? Of course, you do, you invited me."

It was a great night. Before we started, Marie – our guide for the dance – explained the principle of this dance evening and explained that it was a powerful night to celebrate being on Earth. Certain planets were interlinked and were broadcasting strong positive waves of energy to Earth, and by dancing to the songs we would be deeply touched by the energies.

I looked at Mark and we smiled at each other.

"We were each given a candle to light and bless, which were then placed in a large bowl of sand that was duly laid in the centre of the circle. I believe there were nine candles in all."

"That's right, it was a powerful night of dance and joy, and love filled the room. I don't know if you realised it, but I believe you must have felt it, after the second circle dance we were in unison. The steps we took, the words we sang, and the breath all became one. I could see that we became a flower, each of us was a petal, and we became a living, breathing entity. In the next moment I saw a column of blue light fill the centre of the circle. I was floating; we were all floating on this wave of energy. The candles were shining brightly in the centre of the circle and we continued to dance the sacred dance programme. We were elevated. We must have danced nonstop for about an hour, but the last dance was amazing – Nirvana. It came to an end and we just stood, arm in arm, holding the energy of the circle. Marie instructed us to send out a loving thought to someone on Earth or the universe, so that it may help raise the energy. We all stood there in this love consciousness, each following their thought path but collectively one. After some minutes I opened my eyes and gazed down at the candles. Each of the nine candles had almost reached their end. I remember thinking that those were three-hour candles. We had danced for just over an hour and now they were nearly finished. I then understood that the vibration of the circle, the higher consciousness of love had made the candles burn much, much quicker than usual. The fire, earth and air spirits must have been so happy too. Now that's eternity in action."

"You are spot on their Ralph."

The fire had burned down to almost nothing. I had no idea what time it was, nor did it matter, but I felt sleepy.

"Well, I'm off to be in the stars Mark, sleep well."

I rose to my feet, we embraced, and headed for our beds.

I woke up to the sunlight kissing my feet. I must have kicked the quilt to one side during the night, but I had slept deeply. I could hear Mark preparing the table for breakfast in his usual peaceful manner. I was indeed blessed to be on earth with a strong soul mate. Over the years we had supported each other. We were mirrors of each other. I could see so much of me in him and him in me. It made no difference what was occurring in our lives. We simply accepted the situation, who we were, and then sought ways to move forward in a positive way. I truly felt we were in tune with each other, and life, from a soul perspective.

I washed and dressed and made my way to the breakfast table. We greeted each other and then sat down for a late breakfast.

Mark opened the conversation and asked: "Where

are you off to next on your global travels?”

“I’m working on that one; at present I am considering Australia or India. Logically I would choose Australia. I have heard so many stories of the fantastic beaches and sea life that run along the east coast. You know how I love water and marine life. I have never experienced the coral environment and the Great Barrier Reef must be the tops! From the heart prospective I feel that India is pulling me.”

“Why India, Ralph? It’s supposed to be tough there, the environment and the extreme poverty and millions of people.”

“‘You’re right but I want to experience the spirituality of the country, the people and their culture. For example, what is a guru? I have heard from and met so many who have talked of it and have experienced it for themselves. I feel the time will come if it is right for me, so I will keep listening and try to read the signs. If it’s right I am sure I will go to one or the other. But for now, I am here sitting in a Welsh cottage drinking tea and eating toast and marmalade with my spirit brother. How blessed I am?”

“As eternal beings, there is all the time in the world, right?”

“I considered his remark for a moment, then responded: “That’s very logical of you Mark.”

“You’re right Ralph, I have to try to feel what I say rather than just talk.”

“What you just said is the logical way of escaping the responsibility each of us has, to follow a divine path, one of spirituality. I believe that with every breath we take there is an opportunity. Every second is in fact a lifetime. That’s all there ever is, one moment to the next, each one an eternity in itself.”

“Is this our last breakfast then Ralph?”

“In one sense it is, because within each moment there

is life and death. When I have consumed my breakfast there is a death. I will never have the exact same experience ever again; each moment is unique unto itself. That's the meaning of life for me, which is eternity, a never-ending journey of discovery, the expansion of consciousness, and the growth of soul!"

We lifted our teacups simultaneously and made a toast to life!

# Chapter 10

## Being True

It was late autumn, and I woke up realising that the more I thought I knew about life and my part in it, the less I knew. I felt that I must follow a deeper path, do more inner cleansing and transform any shadows that remained. Anything that was blocking my soul expression was not true to universal law. It felt the passion to experience and understand more deeply how universal laws are applied. Thus far I felt that I had gained some valuable insight and experiences that had accelerated my spiritual growth, but I wanted to live completely in truth; "a life without a shadow", no negativity, no fear and no ego.

From what I had read and experienced much is talked about physical evolution from a logical perspective, as in Darwinism, which I felt was animalistic and not a true account of how humans evolved. I knew deep within my being that the human being did not evolve through natural selection, i.e., only the strongest survive. That science has been proven by the same sciences of geology and anthropology to be incorrect. However there remains a resistance, a denial even by many anthropologists and physicists to accepting the undeniable proof. Why? Below, I summarise how I believe the system of logical consciousness operates within its own paradigm, which to my understanding entraps those who do not have the will or vision to look outside of the box. I know this to be true because I was one such person:

## The conscious flow of Logical reasoning

## Everything starts with an

### IDEA

then comes

### THEORY

followed by

### BELIEF

**Theory and belief are only correct until proven wrong**. History shows how fear of change can often cause us to resist change. Why? Because the ego wants to be in control. The Ego and fear are the root causes of this resistence. These two – ego & fear – combined are responsible for controlling a system that is abundant in the societies that have been created out of logic. If the sciences and the hierarchical establishments that are built around them were to admit the undeniable truth, those structures, such as Darwin's Theory of Evolution would collapse. History would then evolve in a new light; a new paradigm shift would take place

As is illustrated above, change can at times feel hard to accept, but time cannot be turned back, it continues to flow, as do the energies that create the Earth. The ego and vanity are well recorded throughout history, and one of the most well-known is that of "King Canute" and the tale of the incoming tide. According to legend, Canute's courtiers flattered him into believing that his word was so powerful that even the tide would recede at his command. Canute is said to have taken this compliment literally and had his throne placed by the shore, where he vainly attempted to command the waves to recede until he almost drowned. I use the tide symbolically in relation to the growing tide of proof that humans did not evolve from Monkeys or Apes.

I have realised from the insights I have been given, that humans were placed on Earth to evolve through spiritual values and that human logical values are but one side of the coin. So, what is the other side showing about whether spirit is as true as is believed by many?

When I explored the experience, I have had from communicating with **true** spirit, the core values were always present; those of Truth, Love, Light, Peace and Joy. I have never ever experienced a **spirit of the light** to be anything other than true and loving. However, I want to share the first experience I had of a spirit entity that had an ego and a dark side. Until this moment I thought that surely Spirit cannot be possessed by darkness, a shadow. This reminds me of the old proverb, 'without a shadow of doubt'. This proverb demonstrates clearly that when you do not doubt yourself there is no shadow to confuse you. The shadow in this respect is fear!

I will take you back several years to when I first discovered that there were false spirit beings. That experience is vividly flooding back to me now. I was very new to visualisation methods at the time, but felt I knew enough to help others on their spiritual path. I was sat in my small therapy room guiding someone called Dina to connect with her main spiritual guide.[15]

---

15 This is a higher being that has been by your side from birth, waiting for you to develop spiritually so that they may assist you in your spiritual development when your three higher senses have been activated.

I felt that Dina was advanced enough to explore this line of communication. I could see that her third eye and throat chakras were active. As a meditation teacher it was my place to hold the space keeping it clear and strong during the mediation.

We went through the relaxation and began the channelling process. On my instructions Dina asked for her main guide to join her. Within a few minutes she felt that there was someone present, standing to her left and just behind her. I asked Dina to ask the spirit being to come closer to her, which it did. She said she felt it was a Native American Indian, so I asked her to ask the spirit for its name. The name *Wolf Man* came to her immediately. Good, I thought to myself. At this point I could not directly visualise the spirit being. I went deeper to access the vibration that the spirit being was on. Within a moment or two I had my vision of him.

"Okay", I said to Dina. "Try to start a dialogue with your main guide. For example, ask what Indian Nation he is from."

"Cherokee", came the reply from Dina.

"'Good, stay with it. Now him ask how he can help you."

There was a long silence. I could see that the spirit guide was fading away but then came back for a few minutes before fading away completely. In that moment I felt that there was something wrong with the communication, but I could not put my finger on it. I asked Dina to return and to open her eyes when she felt fully present. I asked her how she felt about the link to her main guide. She did not seem so sure, so I asked: "Did you feel that this was true for you?"

"I am not 100% sure, I can't put my finger on it, but no, it felt uncomfortable for me."

"Let's see how it goes for you the next time, shall we?"

"Yes, okay. When shall we meet again?"

"How about in three days, same time, same place."

"Fine", said Dina.

I then suggested that she should try to communicate with her main guide in her own time. After Dina had left, I went back into the meditation to explore where the main guide was coming from. I drew a blank, nothing appeared for me, which I felt was strange. After all, Spirit must be true, nothing is hidden with Spirit, or so I thought.

Three days later, Dina arrived promptly for her next guided meditation. We sat down and I immediately asked her how she was doing with her new link to Spirit? Her response was not joyous.

"Well, I have tried a couple of times to get closer to my guide, which worked for the first time, but on the second occasion he began to demand things of me."

"What kind of things?"

"Yes, well, he wanted me to do things. I won't go into any details."

"Well, that's not right. A true spirit never demands anything from anyone; they have no need of anything. This is not OK. If it's alright with you, I would like us to go into a meditation for you to invite this guide back into your space, I will check it out. Is that alright with you?"

Dina nodded her head in agreement, but I detected a bit of fear in her. We went into the meditation and sure enough the main guide was there, he seemed to be stronger in his presence. I asked Dina to simply hold the link and do nothing; I would manage it from here on in. This was a new experience for me, so I asked for guidance from my own guide about what to do next. I was informed to challenge the spirit's identity, so naively I asked it where it came from. Was it a true spirit? The Spirit looked at me and tried to take charge of my psyche, to overpower me, and my influence on the communication. I realised that this was in fact, a false guide, a dark energy that was pretending to be in the light, but when faced with truth, love, and light, could not remain in it. Intuitively I followed the spirit as it tried to run from me. I eventually managed to hold it in the light, from where I could read its mind and obtain insight as to why it was in the dark and not evolving.

I was shown a past life where he was a Native American Indian again. He had murdered a friend because he was jealous of him spending more time with a squaw, who had reincarnated and was now sitting in front of me in the room. I continued to hold the false guide in the light waiting for the next move to come to me. Then it came, and I told the false guide: *"You must get back onto the right path, and work with the negative karma you have created, it's the only way that you will step out of the black belt[16] you find yourself in."*

It's a matter of applying the correct spiritual will. He looked at me long and hard, and said: *"I accept your guidance."*

In that moment, a beam of light came down and I consciously lifted him into it. In a second he was gone. Dina felt it because she physically jerked her body. I asked Dina to return. We opened our eyes and smiled at each other.

"It's over now, he's gone."

"Thank you, Ralph, I knew he was not a true spirit."

We talked for a long time about her relationship with the false guide. She already knew of him from previous mediums, who had stated that there was something interfering with her vibration, and that it must be cleared for it to move on in life.

"Well, it seemed that we met for this reason. Isn't it wonderful how the universe brings people together to

---

16 A negative belt of energy where all dark forces reside when they choose not to follow the path of karma and reincarnate to transform anything negative they have created.

158

clear out what is not true."

Dina agreed, and thanked me for the work I had done on her energy-fields. After she left, I sat down in the therapy room to contemplate what I had just experienced. I realised that I had just given an exorcism. The false main guide had a link into Dina's psyche and was interfering with her vibration, which was why I helped to transform it.

Freedom of choice is another universal law, which is why a true spirit will never demand anything of you or anyone else. This is a universal law.

Some points of reference to support understanding: The reference of all you have experienced on Earth is carried into the next realm.

- You reincarnate with all you have ever been in your many lifetimes. Every experience and thought is with you now from all past lives.
- Those souls who are working on their spiritual development return under the Law of Karma.
- Those souls who – for whatever reason – choose not to return to Earth, under the Law of Karma, reside in what I term The Underworld .[17]
- The same principles are true throughout this universe.

When a physical being is not true to the light, they carry it in their spirit and soul bodies also. Using the example above, in relation to the false guide, that soul had decided to step back into the light and be true to its path, and then the shadow could be transformed as

---

17 This is a belt of dark energy that is close to Earth. It's where all dark souls return when they choose not to follow the light as physical death occurs. They have equal opportunity to step into the light, in order to transform any negative karma, but many do not and remain destructive and possessive.

it passed into the higher light vibration.

Truth cannot be altered or changed. What is hidden will eventually reappear in the light of truth. If I were not true to myself, I will not be true to others. What is **my** truth, may be different from your interpretation of what you feel to be true. But if both are true there will be peace, love, and joy between us. That truth will carry us both to the same place, as all rivers lead to the ocean. This is shown in positive ways when people have a religious following. For example, Christianity refers to it as God, Islam as Allah, Judaism as YHWH.

The negative aspect of this is, when religious groups believe that their God or deity is the one and only True one. That for me is not religion, it is pure EGO, which sadly, is where the majority of religious institutions operate today. It is a growing phenomenon. Where the motto used to be "peace not war", today it's the opposite, "war then peace".

# Chapter 11

# Earth Consciousness

After over a decade following the path of spirituality, it still felt that I had barely scratched the surface. Yes, I had learnt to be present. Yes, my three higher senses were developed to the point that it was like I had a switch, that was directly connected to my clairvoyance, clairaudience, and clairsentience. I could turn them on and off at will. I had been giving spiritual healing for more than a decade now. I had also worked intensely with Mother Earth, with land and property healing, but still I felt that there was something missing. It was like a wave that would come, only to fade away. "Maybe that's how it is. The universe is preparing me in its own way; it's in the ethers but has not yet materialised." I decided to sit and meditate on the subject to be free of logical interference. Within the next few minutes, I was at my rendezvous, meeting my main guide. We duly greeted each other and began to converse telepathically:

"You have seen what I am currently working on?"

*"Yes, and I have also sensed that you are holding some frustration."*

"You are of course correct in your observation. Is there anything you do not know or cannot see about me or indeed the universe?"

*"In regard to you, there is nothing that can be hidden. The universe is another matter. Sometimes it is required to journey much deeper, to journey beyond its consciousness, to obtain the wisdom. Universal laws are truly universal. What is true for me is also true for you; it's a matter of frequency, vibration, light. You are now trying to access higher knowledge[18] to meet the true Self, and one aspect of your development is learning to remain in the Love Ray at all times. This is what we are doing now, communicating through love. You are simply remembering who you are."*

"That is so true. What is memory anyway? No, let's get back to what I wanted to share with you in relation to astral travel and seeking knowledge. Some six years ago I went to see a trance medium with Mark. Oops, back into the time thing again. Anyway, it was a private sitting by invitation only. I had never seen a trance medium working, but Mark had. It was a short journey to the location, some thirty minutes or so, and we arrived in good time. We walked along a stone pathway which led to a beautiful garden resting behind an old country cottage. It was a late summer evening, and the sun was disappearing over the horizon. Even at this late season there were many flowers displaying their beauty, particularly the roses, ah the perfume. There was even a small pond with a few Carp in it. It was a serene place. We met our hosts Rhian and Dafydd, who I felt to be very warm and caring. The rest of the group, nine in all, were quietly engaged in their own conversations. In the next moment everyone intuitively moved into the hallway of the house. Mark hung our coats and followed the group into what must have been the main room, which was large enough to sit everyone. Tea was being served, as

---

18 A vibration of consciousness that exceeds logical limitations.

is the tradition in Wales. Mark and I knew two of the people there. We were then introduced to the trance medium Elisabeth, and her husband John. She was a spritely lady, young in heart and mind. Her husband stood back a bit; I felt, as a mark of respect. Everyone found their seats as John accompanied Elisabeth into another room to prepare for her trance.

The energy in the room was electric to say the least. Some fifteen minutes or more must have passed, when I heard Elisabeth making her way into the room, closely followed by John. I could not help but notice as she walked past me that her stance had totally changed. She was leaning to her left and was bent over holding a stick with a slightly shaky left hand. The aura of the room was amazing to feel and see, I have rarely felt such stillness amongst people. Elisabeth, or whoever it was, raised her head slightly, her face had become oriental looking. She introduced herself as *Al Lam* and duly welcomed us in a most humbling manner. She spoke in broken English with what I believed to be a distinct Chinese accent. Her very presence was so powerful, and felt as if she was coming from a deep place. The wisdom she shared was clear and precise, and enlightening.

She must have talked for over an hour and was now closing her wonderful presentation of universal laws. Al Lam then invited those present to ask any question they might have. Three of the group asked specific questions in relation to their personal life, which were answered in an astounding manner; giving different view of life from an enlightened viewpoint. I had prepared a couple of my own questions, but after her presentation I felt them inappropriate. I had already received the answers, but then, she once again invited questions. I went deep within, then there rose a question and I said: "Yes, I have one please." I presented my question, and then a deep silence settled in the room. After a few moments Al Lam replied: "That is an interesting question. Please wait a minute, I must go and find the answer. I will be back shortly." Al Lam was motionless; I felt that she was journeying to another place to find the answer. Some minutes passed, then I saw a very slight glow of light passing into her and she moved slightly, with a twitching movement. Then she was back. She responded to my question in the same manner as she had to the others. I now understood, and she said: "Thank you for that. It was an interesting journey for me." I bowed to her in respect and she then closed the service and retreated to the other room to restore herself as Elisabeth.

The room was vibrating in serenity and love. The whole group seemed to be in a trance like state. What we had experienced, or for me at least, was astounding. Her voice held a power that I had not felt before. The closest word I can find to describe it is absolute. I could tell that Mark was also taken back, and that's saying something. Mark is very deep and is not fooled in any way by anyone. He picked up my thoughts and turned to me saying: "That was amazing, I have no words."

We stood there in silence for a moment, then Elisabeth and John re-entered the room. There she was as I had first met her, spritely once again. Everyone greeted her with a warm smile, some I felt not knowing how to handle who she was now. I waited for the right moment to talk with her. I glided through the group hearing their thoughts on the presentation by Al Lam.

Then there came the moment and I went to talk with Elisabeth – Al Lam. She had such strength in her eyes,

they were shining. I asked her: "What does your name
Al Lam mean?"

"It translates in English to Peace."

"That is you, for sure. I want to thank you for answering my question."

"Which one was that?"

"The one where you had to journey to another place
to receive the answer."

"Ah, it was yours", came her immediate reply.

"It was then I knew that she was a true channel because she did not know who had asked the question. If
she, Al Lam, had in any form or manner been logical,
it would have been Elisabeth speaking and ego based,
but no, her truth was universally empowering. I once
again thanked her for her service to Spirit, the group,
and left her presence with a deep sense of gratitude.
My question to you is this. Where did she go to find
the answer?"

*"I feel that I am repeating myself here, which often
happens to appease the logic. Everything is known
in the universe, but this is not the only universe in
existence, as vast as it may seem to logic. There are
countless universes. If you can imagine that each
universe is like a cell in your body, and that cell is
connected to all other cells. This is the matrix that's
often referred to when people talk of the interconnection of universal consciousness. Now when one
cell wants to know what another cell is doing in the
matrix, it may take a little bit longer to get there,
depending on where that knowledge is. That is why
Al Lam was away for a few minutes, the soul had to
journey to a far-off universe to receive the knowledge and the answer to your question."*

I could not help but interrupt: "But wait a minute,

does that mean that some of the universal laws of this universe are actually from another universe?"

*"Yes, they are, and yet not. It would help if you could consciously keep in mind, the thought that we are all one body of energy, so what applies here also applies in other universes in accordance with what it requires to keep it healthy and light. For example, your heart and liver are in different areas of the body, but they have different functions; same body, different functions. The universe operates under the same laws."*

"So, she, I mean Al Lam, journeyed to another part of the cosmic body or infinite universal bodies?"

*"That's somewhere approaching the truth."*

"Wow, that is a mind stopper. Wherever she went for the answer it was certainly compelling and I am eternally grateful."

*"You are welcome. I hear you have another question?"*

"I am trying to understand more deeply the relation of Earth's energy to this universe, and why so many souls are drawn to be here."

*"You have brothers and sisters in a given number of universes that are of the light seed of God."*

"Can you please elaborate?"

*"What I will say is this. There are a given number of universes within God consciousness and those universes are governed by the laws that continue to maintain the vibration of love and light. It is these very laws that created your very being, from head - soul to foot – physical self. That's why you sometimes use the words 'from head to toe' to describe*

*when something is complete, covered from head to toe."*

"What about the ones outside of God consciousness, are they alien or dangerous?"

*"Some are extremely alien, but there is a protective system in place to prevent alien forces from entering."*

"Can you talk more about this?"

*"I will keep it simple. You know that you have an aura. That is your personal protective energy field and this is how it operates. Your physical body and brain can only receive a certain amount of light, which emanates from your star, the sun. Now that light is atomic in nature, but as soon as the light touches your aura and passes through it, it is transformed from an atomic energy into a sub-atomic energy, a lower vibration. From there the sub-atomic energy passes through the etheric body, which is electromagnetic, and then links to your central nervous system. You remember me informing you that we are built in the image of God; well, the Earth is like an organ in your physical body. It has an aura, which you call 'the ozone layer'. The ozone filters much of the gamma rays or photons, which are the most energetic and dangerous forms of physical light, and the most harmful to the human cell, particularly the DNA. So, as you may begin to understand, there is an order to things. The chaos theory does not see the whole picture, just one aspect of it.*

*To answer your question more fully, the universe also has an aura, similar to Earth and yourself. The universal aura is preventing alien energies from entering, and those that do, do not last. Again, refer-*

*ring to yourself and your physical body, what happens when a negative energy enters your space, or to be more precise your aura? You immediately feel its presence in some form or other, and if it comes from behind, you may automatically turn around to see what is there. That's your intuition telling you that an alien energy is nearby. Now, take that a step closer to the physical body, particularly your immune system. Look what happens when an alien energy enters your body; your 'antibodies' set to work to destroy them. Well, the same principle applies to the universal body of light; any darkness cannot remain; only those of the light can live in such an environment, that's the law."*

"So you're saying that the light is my greatest protector?"

*"Absolutely!"*

"I have no words."

*"I have one last point to make in relation to the aura, which I feel is vital for your spiritual growth. You create your own 'space' around you. This is basically the consciousness you are holding within your aura. The higher the consciousness the more positive it is, meaning that anything negative would find it extremely difficult to enter such an environment. So, who is it that lets other people's negativity into your space? It's important to understand how things happen, and what it means, but do not hold any negative energy any longer than identifying it, otherwise, it becomes yours, which can confuse your own psyche. Anything negative you create, which could be a thought or an emotion, will disturb your natural harmonious balance. The ego is the master of cre-*

*ating negativity through judgment, fear, needs and expectations. I believe you now have a much clearer picture of your responsibility to maintain a positive life force on all levels."*

"I must have some space to absorb everything you have told me .... So, Earth is indeed a living breathing energy. No wonder the Native Americans refer to the earth as Mother Earth. She is indeed alive but not in good shape at present. What more can I do to help balance her?"

*"You have done much already. Keep listening to Gaia and she[19] will come to you in some form or other. I will step back for now, dear brother."*

My guide faded away like a white mist into the darkness and was gone but yet, so close.

§

I spent the next few days contemplating and meditating on the guidance and knowledge I had received in relation to earth consciousness and universal laws. I was beginning to understand on a deeper level how important the work I had done so far was on rebalancing the land. The ley-lines and magnetic vortexes were created to keep Earth healthy and vibrant. I realised that they were equivalent to the meridians and minor chakra points in the physical body. I was shown that mystics such as Merlin had been using ley-lines as a transcendental link from one place to another. He used them to travel all over Britain and possibly the world because everyone is linked into the grid. So, the magnetic field around the Earth is helping to ground the universal consciousness by dropping the higher vibration of light into a conscious vibration; giving hu-

---

19  Gaia is Mother Nature, or the planet Earth.

mans the first aspect of consciousness, logic.

I sat down to go a bit deeper into my thoughts, then there was a beautiful picture building up in front of me like an aurora of colour and light that were creating images of a divine shimmering place. I closed my eyes to go deeper into what I was now experiencing. In a flash I was travelling through the universe at an incredible speed. Stars were flashing past my periphery and I knew I was going somewhere deep into the cosmos. Suddenly, I stopped, bang, like I had slammed into an invisible wall, but not hurt in the least. It felt like I was floating somewhere but where was I? It was like the darkest night; I couldn't see a thing. It was pitch black. Then I consciously put out a thought: "Where am I?" Then I telepathically received a question.

*"What would you like?"*

"I would like to have some trees."

A forest of tall spruce trees appeared in front of me.

*"Is there anything else you would like?"*

"Yes, a stream."

The stream was there just before me. I could hear it trickling as it ran over the rocks. There were some brown trout bathing in the sunlight, everything was glistening, it was so beautiful.

*"And something else?"*

"I have always wanted to live in a log cabin. Could I have one?"

In a flash it was there to my left. I stood there mesmerised by it all. The telepathy started again.

*"You may now realise on a deeper level that what you think, you create. This is your reality just as it is mine."*

"I do, I do, I do and thank you for this powerful lesson. I am the creator of my own life through consciously applying it, not needlessly but with respect. I returned to my physical body and was overcome with happiness, as tears ran down my cheeks."

§

There was an intense period of four days, just studying my thoughts. Looking at how I had wanted to have certain things, the materialism of need and the need to consume, have more. I really had been programmed on how to behave and live, but that was in the past and this was now. There was an intense feeling of peace within. It felt like I was resting from the stress that materialism creates. It became clearer to me, why so many had fought for their freedom and liberty to do what they wished. But I saw another side to it, which was the illusion that had been created around freedom, because ultimately, I *am* free. Someone may want to kill my body, but they sure cannot take my soul, now that is my definition of freedom - no fear.

I took myself off to bed. There was need to count sheep tonight. I fell asleep in a moment. At sometime early the next morning I entered a vision. In the vision I was being guided to work on some land in specific areas, three in all. I was guided to use my pendulum in certain areas to pinpoint their location, and then to do the work. I sat up quickly and opened my eyes. How interesting. I quickly got out of bed, washed, and dressed in no time at all. It was 7.30 a.m. After making the statutory cup of tea I opened the ordinance survey map for the local area. I found the rough areas that I had been shown and began to use the pendulum to work out the exact position of the ley-lines that were requiring my attention. It never ceases to amaze me with how the pendulum works. It is a matter of magnetism and polarity. For example, I was looking for a precise spot on the map. I sent out the thought that was focused to find the vortex in a specific place on the map and I asked the pendulum to give me a *yes* answer (turning anticlockwise in my case), as I went over the general area on the map. Sure enough, the pendulum turned anticlockwise and it was located. Then I worked out where the next point was and then the third one. Then the triangle was complete, three magnetic vortexes and three ley-lines. All ley-lines start from a vortex of energy to from a triangle. When all three vortex points are positive, everything living within the triangle would resonate on a positive energy. But if the energy had been corrupted of damaged by negative energies then the energy within the triangle would be negative.

It took me another ninety minutes to work it all out. I got my tools together and sped off on the Triumph. The first location was some eighteen miles south-east from my place. The second link, or vortex, was fifteen miles due west and the third link was due north, some twelve miles. This was a big one, the biggest yet. The second triangle was even bigger and took much of the afternoon to work on. I looked up at the sun and estimated it was six in the afternoon. With one more to do, I headed for the coast not far from where I lived. On arrival I recognised where I was. I had taken some walks along this part of the coast but in the opposite direction down towards a coastal village called Mwnt. I climbed a long hill and located the first spot, worked on it, and duly moved to the second one. It was a beautiful evening, clear blue skies, the ocean was in front of me with a long drop to the shore bellow.

An hour or more must have passed before I headed for the last of the three fix points. It was quite rocky where I stood but fortunately it did not hinder the work. This last triangle was rather small compared to the two previous ones and I was trying to find out its significance. There was a small lighthouse not far from where I stood; maybe it had something to do with that, a kind of invisible light that would warn anyone of danger? I placed the last crystal into the ground and I had finished. I stood on the spot to feel the new energies that were now emanating from this triangle. It felt clear, strong, and free from any negativity. In the next moment I looked up into the clear blue sky and out from the sky there came floating towards me a large white feather. I opened my hand to catch it. I held it next to my heart and knew that this was a gift from Spirit, a mark of respect for the day's work; it's as simple as that.

# Chapter 12

# Living from the Heart

After spending over a year giving therapy and running meditation classes at a Shiatsu training centre in Germany, I had returned to Wales and was staying with my spirit brother Mark. A friend contacted me to ask if I would be interested in helping to organise a healing circle at a music festival in Pembrokeshire called "Dance Camp Wales". The group would give therapy throughout the festival. It felt right and I immediately said yes. It would be a great place to be for some eight days.

I had previously been to this annual event a couple of times in the last four years. There was so much love, joy, and peace there; soul to soul meetings, good food, great workshops and music of all kinds. Mark had kindly offered to drive me there, which was great, but that was still a few days away. Right now, I felt I wanted to go more deeply into the meaning of self-love through self-observation. For me love was being egoless because ego is selfish not self-less. My experiences thus far were always pointing towards transforming the egos identity, into the *Self* and eventually *Being*.

I knew that within, there was a spiritual force, a power whose whole purpose was ultimately to transform the *I* within me. I was now passing through the *Self*, the nonattachment, so that I could *Be!* The words "*Human Being*" is a duality; human is the form side and being is formless. By being I was in a timeless non-material space, not locked into form and identity of the egoic *I*.

I was only too willing to learn to live harmoniously, through applying the consciousness that would establish this deeper sense of being. I had faith that my soul and spirit would continue to lead me along the pathway of transformation, and if I woke up every morning there must be more to do. Living, breathing, and expressing my truth gave me greater peace within. Right now, I felt that I was in a good space of Self; one of cheerful co-operation. I was now living a life where my spiritual-will never compromised the ego, because I had no fear, need or desire; my motives being pure and clear. The spiritual guidance I had received until this moment had been invaluable in helping me develop a sustained positive frame of mind. I literally felt that my consciousness was expanding and receiving greater light.

The next day I awoke, followed my instincts to head for Penbryn Beach, which had a beautiful long stretch of sand, rocks and cliffs. It was mid-June and warm. I turned off the A4971 and headed towards the coast along a single track road that passed through a small valley leading to the beach. There was a spectacular display of countless shades of green, deciduous trees; including ash, oak, sycamore and even some beech lining the sides of the road. It was breath-taking.

On arrival at the car park, I pulled the Triumph onto its stand and headed for the beach. It was practically deserted, apart from a few people in the distance. As I walked along, I remained in what was becoming a natural awakened state of spirituality. I was in a space that was void of time. I was totally relaxed, everything was as one, the sea, sky, birds, sand and rock, no separation. I stopped for a moment and took off my boots and socks and felt the warm sand beneath my feet. I paused for a moment to reflect upon the energy of the sand. I looked beyond the sand, as I had when I had studied holographic pictures. I could see that the sand was moving; each grain was energy unto itself. I was frozen on the spot, mesmerised by my experience. My mind started to process the experience and it began to fade, so I blocked my logic, and simply observed in a no-mind space with my spiritual eye. Then the full experience returned, and my physical view adjusted to this new experience. I could see that each grain was vibrating which gave the impression of it finding the right place for it to be. It reminded me of when I cuddled up to someone; nesting into that space to feel comfortable. The sand was doing the same thing but on a minute scale. I reflected that it was alive; the mineral kingdom is a living organism.

I bent down and gently moved some sand with my right hand and lifted some up for it to flow through my fingers. It felt so alive, so energised by the sunlight and when I walked upon it with bare feet, I took in all that energy, through my feet. Now I knew why I always like walking barefoot on sandy beaches. I took the next step forward towards the wet stretch of sand before me. Ahead, was a large rock jutting out of the sand near to the rippling water's edge. Sitting on the rock, I continued to hold the energy of being present. I felt the vibration of every sound and the colour of its essence, the beauty of its being, the physical energy of light. My heart was full; nature filled my very being with its essence. I beheld the spirit of love through nature, it spoke to me, caressed my etheric energy with its waves of colour. I was in an enlightened moment, staying with each moment, a timeless being. Everything continued to be, following the timeless rhythm.

A couple walked past and noticed my presence but did not approach. I observed their gentle smile as they gazed upon my joy of being and walked by in silence like ships passing in the night, aware but not attached.

I rose to my feet and started to walk back to my motorbike. It felt as if I was in the holographic energy and was simply observing life around me, literally walking through it and yet not directly attached to it. Was I dreaming? Was I really in the here and now? Then what is real? Now I felt I was becoming lost in the consciousness of logic, trying to justify everything, put it into boxes, units of what fits what. A moment of reflection came to me. Everything is an illusion when you have stepped out of it, but when you are in it, you are following its flow and you do not realise that you are in that space of nothingness. I continued with this self-processing. This must be what a walking meditation is like; fully present and experiencing life in that vibration. Now I understood; it's a matter of applied consciousness. Simply being in the moment creates a vacuum, a space where anything is possible. This took me back to the experience of creating my own reality of space; the trees, the brook, the log cabin.

I got back to Mark's place and I shared my experiences of the beach with him. He was fascinated with what I had described and decided he would experiment for himself, the next time he was on a beach.

It was festival time, and I was packed and ready to go. Over breakfast Mark was asking all kinds of questions about Dance Camp Wales. He had heard me talk of it before but at that time he was not so interested, so I gave him a general picture of the event, which increased his interest. It was a sunny Friday morning and the weather forecast for the week was good, but I never took much notice of the weather predictions. I had learnt that in this part of the world the weather was localised, and as such was beyond prediction within a day or two.

An hour later we arrived at the entrance gate of the field where the festival was taking place. It was the day before the opening day because the healing circle had to be organised and a sacred space set up. June, the owner of the dairy farm and organiser, was stood next to a ten-man tent near the entrance. We got out of the car and June and I greeted each other with a warm embrace. I introduced Mark and she then pointed to the area where the healing circle would be. The camp field was about fifteen acres in size and gently sloped down towards a small, wood covered ravine through which ran a stream. I could see the healing area was in the bottom right-hand corner.

After some moments of sharing, Mark and I got back into the car, and made our way around the various main tents that were already standing.

A small circle of therapy tents was already in place and I was welcomed by my friend Gwen who was a nurse and another of the organisers. The other two therapists were Mac, a psychologist, and Peter who practiced classical massage. We had worked together at the two previous events and it was great to see them again. I grabbed my rucksack from Marks's car and looked for a suitable spot to set up my tent. I put my camp gear down and we were invited to sit and have some tea by the open fire with some hot water that was on the go.

An hour later another healer called Steve joined us, he was the youngest and had just qualified in Shiatsu. Gwen told us that there would be three other newly qualified Shiatsu students joining the group tomorrow. My friend Mark decided to leave us, and I went to the gate where we said our goodbye's for now. I spent the rest of the day meeting others and generally socialising.

There was one circus type tent which served as the main tent and five other smaller ones which were housing other activities like drum journeys and circle dancing. The food and canteen area were based at the top left of the field, looking from the healing area. In previous years it had been a hive of activity and a popular meeting place. In a small, wooded area behind me, some 50 yards away, was a permanent wood and brick-built fire tunnel which was for the sauna.

After setting up my tent I headed for the sauna as soon as I saw that there was smoke coming out of the chimney. I just wanted to be in stillness after so much talking. As I was approaching the sauna, I saw a guy loading the fire chamber with some large logs. I stopped for a moment to watch him working; he was totally engrossed in the task at hand. When he had filled the chamber, he securely closed its door, stood up and wiped his sweaty brow. Then he noticed me standing there, just a few feet away.

"Oh! I did not see you", he said surprised.

I went to shake his hand and introduced myself. The fire guardian was Zac and he had travelled all the way down from the borders between England and Scotland.

"You were here a few years ago weren't you?" I asked.

"That's right. Can't keep me away, I love it here; something to do with the people and the energy it creates. It's addictive. Never thought I would be addicted to anything in my life, but this place has got to me."

He chuckled as he said the last few words in his broad border accent.

"So this is your Karma Yoga?"[20]

"Yes it is. 24/7 for the duration, and what is yours?" he said as if he knew I was not a paying guest.

"I'm serving in the healing area and give hands on-healing."

"Oh great, I may come and pay you a visit, I have a back problem. Can you fix that sort of thing?"

---

20 Work undertaken to pay for their festival ticket

"Can't say directly, come and visit. It's an open space there, either me or another may be able to give you a treatment."

"Does it cost anything?"

"I work on donations as I believe the others do to."

"I like that, pay or give what you can, it's an exchange isn't it, whether it is a loaf of bread or another treatment in exchange. This is how we should live. You know, I believe money is the root of all evil. How do you feel about that Ralph?"

"You know, I like your directness and being open as you are, and it's true, much misery is created by money. For me, it's not money in itself, it's how it is used. The greed for more for example, the ego cannot get enough of it because to the ego money is power. That for me is where the real problem lies."

I could see that Zac was deep in contemplation as he rubbed the beard stubble on his chin.

"That's a fair point - human greed."

"Well, I think I will go for the sauna."

"Yeah, go for it, man. Should be well hot by now; has been alight all morning. The shower is over there."

"Oh yes, I remember now from the last time I was here, and thanks for taking care of this space, it feels really good here."

"Well yes it's my home too for the next seven days."

"I like the wind chimes, dream catchers and feathers Zac."

He smiled in appreciation.

"Have a good one; catch you later".

And off he went.


I stripped and layed my clothes on the bails of straw that formed a half circle by the side of the sauna. It seemed that there were one or two others in there judging by the clothes that were hanging on a branch.

The sauna itself was homemade and circular in shape. As I entered it took a few minutes for my eyes to get used to the quality of light. As I remembered, there was a small window directly over the fire chamber that ran into the centre of the sauna. On either side of the chamber were the benches, top and bottom, with enough room for about twenty people. Not a big space, but very cosy and it was great to be in this natural environment to just unwind.

I said a brief hi to the two who were already in there and we sat in silence for a long time. Then they left quietly and I was alone. Zac was right it was "well hot" in there, the thermostat read 98C. My eyes had now adjusted to the dim light and I could clearly make out the structure of the oak benches and wild tree branches that formed the protective barrier around the fire. Then I heard someone coming in. It was Gwen and she sat right next to me.

"So, this is where you are. I've been looking for you."

"It's a great space to be, I will be here at least once a day, just in case you can't find me."

We chuckled. and chatted about what had occurred in our lives over the last year since we last met. Then Gwen shared her idea of how we could organise the healing area with so many therapists arriving: "There will be a meeting late tomorrow morning to discuss how things should be run."

"That's fine by me, I look forward to it."

We sat and continued our general discussion for what must have been another hour because Zac had returned to reload the fire. Gwen left before me and I then took a welcome cold shower under the foliage. Heaven on Earth.

Surprisingly, it was already supper time as I heard the mealtime gong ringing, which filled the air. I must have been in the sauna for a long time! With my towel under my arm, I made my way to the eating area. Many more people had arrived; as I noticed that the area allocated for tents was filling up. Each of the Dance Camp Wales festivals that I had attended had approximately two to three thousand festival goers, and this one seemed normal.

There was a modest queue for food, so I joined and stood behind a very colourful African man. He turned to see who was behind him, and we immediately connected and embraced each other like lost brothers. We got our food and sat down to enjoy our meal together.

Later in the week I heard that the teenagers wanted to have an evening of rap music, which was to be held in the main tent, which was put to the vote and it was a positive one for the rappers, which was set for Thursday. They were given a strict time to play the rap music between 7 p.m. and 11 p.m.

On Thursday night I had decided to go into the sauna in order to numb the effects this type of music would have on my ears. Sure enough the rap music started to bellow out of the main tent, which was slightly softened by the surrounding fabric of the sauna.

I began to feel this anger rise within me towards the rap music and the more I listened to it the more angry I became. Then I closed my eyes and asked for some insight towards why I was judging the rap music so strongly. Then the word came to me "go into the eye of the storm, on the outside it always seems worse than what it is". I contemplated upon what I had just received for some time; then suddenly I got it, my lesson was about acceptance. I must accept it!

I quickly made my way out of the sauna, took a shower and got dressed in no time. I stood at the entrance of the tent and could see how happy the mixed age of people were, with the majority being teenagers. I stepped in and put my towel to one side and started to dance. A few minutes later I began to loosen the negativity I had towards rap music. As time went on I got more into it and was one of the last to leave. I realised that my judgment of rap music had created a shadow over my energy and that the ego had managed to overpower my consciousness from the time I had begun to resent it. By my entering the storm of rap I went into its eye and from there was able to embrace it instead of rejecting it, and had a great time too!

The next few days just seemed to fly by and on opening my tent it was a bright sunny Sunday morning, as it had been for most of the week. Many of the festival goers were already dismantling their tents, Teepis and some Yurts. I went up to the food tent and sat next to Zac and had some breakfast. We both felt that the festival week had been a great success and we both planned to return next year.

As I was packing my tent some people came to say their goodbyes with much love and joy for the times we had shared. Mark and I had arranged for him to pick me up at noon that day. In no time at all I was ready to go and headed for the camp entrance. I was saying goodbye to June and others when I noticed that Mark had arrived and we headed off to his home.

Mark's home was always open for me to stay for as long as I wanted to. On the second day at Mark's home I had an insight into everything that I had experienced in life up until this present moment: my inner truth was telling me that throughout every trial and hardship that I had experienced, my entire being is sustained by a knowing which transcends all fears because the love of God is present in my heart.

The Divine Spirit has no vested interest in me or you other than to guide us through those shadows we create and into the light of the moment. The inborn love that we hold is waiting and willing to expand, to open like a flower that is kissed by the sunlight. Every human being has the ability to wake up to spiritual realities; because there is only one way to go, which is forward and upwards into a greater light.

The greater plan has been in place for millions of years and every soul in this constellation has a part to play in its evolution. My part is to live in the moment.

Be at peace with myself.

Love all things.

Trust and listen to my inner knowing that gives me insights into what I am experiencing.

Be fearless.

I continue to follow and listen to those wise words to this very day.


*Peace, love and light, Ralph Jenkins*

## About the Author

I am a student of life who continually seeks Universal wisdom. I have the ability to see abstract energies such as the aura and chakras. These gifts enable me to connect and interact with many of the life forces that logic cannot reason with. I explore these insights that connect to metaphysics and various sciences, such as Astrophysics, Quantum mechanics, Physiology and Pathology of the body. All of these are, in my opinion, linked to the essence of life.

I am guided to direct the awareness I have been entrusted to help others, and continually seek opportunities to share my spiritual experiences with others through mutual dialogue.

Energy is often talked about but not felt or experienced in concrete ways. In the light of this I am open to give lectures, seminars and a variety of videos as a means to create greater understanding of Universal Laws.

You can read more about my work at the following websites:

www.verusanimus.com
www.circleoflighthealing.com
www.ghostbusting.se